GENETICALLY MODIFIED LANGUAGE

The GM debate is a war of words, to be won as much by persuasion as by action in the laboratory, field or supermarket. As the argument intensifies and the voices on all sides get louder, *Genetically Modified Language* cuts through the controversy to unpick the issues and ideology at the heart of the debate.

Scientific, commercial, ethical or political perspectives each have their own discourse, with differing styles of argument, metaphors, analogies and word choices. When they are mixed together, either inadvertently or on purpose, this can lead to dramatic misunderstanding and disagreement. By carefully examining the language used by key players in the arena, from the media to politicians, supermarkets, biotech corporations and scientists, Guy Cook analyses critically the effects of their arguments on both policy and opinion.

Written in a clear, accessible style and drawing on illustrative examples, *Genetically Modified Language* is an insightful look at how language shapes, and can be used to manipulate, our opinions.

Guy Cook is Professor of Applied Linguistics at the University of Reading. He has published widely on discourse analysis and the teaching of language and literature. His previous books include *Discourse* (1989), *Discourse and Literature* (1994), *Language Play, Language Learning* (2000) and *The Discourse of Advertising* (second edition, 2001).

This timely book will interest not only those involved in the GM debates, but anyone interested in the public understanding of science, the rhetoric of public discussion of environmental issues, and the relation of technoscientific debates to beliefs and values.

(Greg Myers, Lancaster University)

Using unscientific, emotional, even irrational arguments, GM proponents attack critics as unscientific, emotional, and irrational. The skeptical public, meanwhile, is dismissed as ignorant and misled. Bravo Guy Cook for catching the inconsistent, hypocritical, and close-minded reasoning used to prop up this dangerous technology.

(Jeffrey M. Smith, Author of *Seeds of Deception*)

GENETICALLY MODIFIED LANGUAGE

The discourse of arguments for GM crops and food

Guy Cook

Routledge
Taylor & Francis Group

LONDON AND NEW YORK

First published 2004
by Routledge
2 Park Square, Milton Park, Abingdon, Oxon OX14 4RN

Simultaneously published in the USA and Canada
by Routledge
270 Madison Ave, New York, NY 10016

Routledge is an imprint of the Taylor & Francis Group

© 2005 Guy Cook

Typeset in Bembo by BC Typesetting Ltd, Bristol
Printed and bound in Great Britain by
TJ International Ltd, Padstow, Cornwall

British Library Cataloguing in Publication Data
A catalogue record for this book is available from the British Library

Library of Congress Cataloging in Publication Data
Cook, Guy (Guy W. D.)
Genetically modified language: the discourse of arguments for GM
crops and food/Guy Cook.
p.   cm.
Includes bibliographical references and index.
1. Transgenic plants. 2. Genetically modified foods. 3. Crops–
Genetic engineering–Language. 4. Food–Biotechnology–Language.
5. Discourse analysis. I. Title.
SB123.57.C665 2004
631'.523–dc22   2004005597

ISBN 0–415–31467–4 (hbk)
ISBN 0–415–31468–2 (pbk)

TO THE MEMORY OF MY FATHER

Though bladed corn be lodg'd . . . though the treasure
Of Nature's germens tumble all together
Even till destruction sicken; answer me
To what I ask you.

(*Macbeth*, IV. i. 50–61)

CONTENTS

CONTENTS

ACKNOWLEDGEMENTS

This book would not have been possible without the work of Elisa Pieri. She collected the press archive, conducted the interviews and focus groups, looked up sources, attended innumerable GM 'events', provided the account of the 'GM nation?' debate in Chapter 8, and offered detailed and discerning commentary on everything I have written. I have relied upon her knowledge, advice and encouragement, and have been inspired by her optimism and commitment.

I have also benefited immensely from my collaboration with Peter T. Robbins and learned much from his insights into the politics and sociology of GM. This book owes a great deal to him.

As other friends and colleagues know, I have constantly pestered them for their opinion on what I have written. I appreciate more than I can say that in their very busy lives they nevertheless found time to help, often at very short notice, during the closing stages of writing. In particular, I have relied upon thorough, perceptive and frank advice on the manuscript from Elena Cook, Kieran O'Halloran, Tony Smith and Henry Widdowson. It has been my good fortune also to have drawn upon the friendship and expertise of Greg Myers, Alison Sealey, Malcolm Williams and Brian Wynne.

I thank the ESRC for the grants which made possible the two consecutive research projects reported in Chapters 2, 3 and 8: 'The presentation of GM crop research to non-specialists: a case study' (R/000/22/3725), November 2001–November 2002; and 'The discourse of the GM food debate: how language choices affect public trust' (RES/000/22/0132), January–December 2003.

I am grateful to Sue Mayer for advice on some of the scientific detail in Appendix 1, and to Malise Ruthven for advice on my discussion of Islamic theology (though any remaining errors in either are my own).

Lastly, my thanks to Louisa Semlyen, Christy Kirkpatrick and Kate Parker at Routledge for their unfailing efficiency and friendliness, and to Rosamund Howe for correcting and greatly improving the manuscript.

The following institutions and individuals have kindly given permission to reprint materials:

Clarence House for 'My 10 fears for GM food', by the Prince of Wales, *Daily Mail*, 1 June 1999.

Monsanto for extracts from 'Monsanto's Pledge' © 2002 Monsanto Company. Reproduced with permission of Monsanto Company.

News International Syndication for extracts from 'Isn't there a chemical spray for Meacher blight?' by Mick Hume, *The Times*, 17 February 2003.

The Royal Society for extracts from Lord May's anniversary address, 2002 © The Royal Society.

Every effort has been made to trace and contact copyright holders. The publishers would be pleased to hear from any copyright holders not acknowledged here so that this acknowledgements page can be amended at the earliest opportunity.

INTRODUCTION

Genetically modified plants will change the nature of life on Earth.

As a general statement, this is something on which both proponents and opponents might agree. But their interpretations of this sentence would be very different. For proponents, GM will fight plant pests, lessen environmental damage, combat world hunger, improve nutrition, and create 'tastier fruits and vegetables'.[1] For opponents, it will damage wildlife, create new health risks, exploit poor farmers, undermine democracy, and disrupt Nature – without bringing any benefits.

Along with many others, this book critically analyses the case for GM. Uniquely, though, rather than simply rehearsing the arguments, it focuses upon the language being used, and goes into minute detail about apparently trivial choices of wording. It is written in the belief that understanding how people talk and write about GM can be as important to making up our minds about it as the scientific facts; and, more generally, that such analysis can provide crucial insights into the nature of power, conflict and decision-making in the contemporary world.

Why language? And why focus upon apparently trivial details of its use? An analogy may help. One purpose of a window is to show us the world outside, so that we can gather information about what is going on there. So when we look through a window we do not usually focus upon the pane, but through it. To rest our eyes on a smudge on the glass would seem foolish, especially if there was something important, and potentially dangerous to us, happening outside.

Language could seem in some ways comparable: one of its functions is to convey information about the world. We treat it as a transparent medium through which we perceive important facts and ideas. Thus, when deciding on a course of action, we feel we should be interested,

1

quite reasonably and practically, in *what* people are saying rather than *how* – on what is beyond, rather than on, the glass.

The window pane of language, however, is far from being clear and clean. It is often smudged, or curved in ways which distort the images beyond. We may even begin to feel that there is no clear division between the window and the world beyond, and that although there *is* an independent reality being talked about, the particular window which someone has placed in front of us is creating the world we see, rather than simply providing access to it. In the daily run of things, this may not always matter. We know that everyone has their own particular way of perceiving things and talking about them. We build that into our understanding. We still get a general view of what they mean. But there are also occasions when the language distorts what it purports to describe in ways which may not be immediately obvious. In these cases, by focusing upon it and by scrutinising it carefully, we get a better idea of what is beyond. Close analysis may help us to separate fact and opinion when they are entangled.

When the talk is about something which will affect our lives profoundly, then such attention to linguistic and logical detail (rather as in a legal document) can be very important indeed. There are times when we simply cannot let ourselves be carried along, vaguely acquiescing in what is said. The glass of language through which we see GM crop technology is just such a case, and one which demands our attention.

This book aims to show that many arguments for GM exemplify disturbing trends in the public use of contemporary English by powerful individuals and organisations, in which language, while purporting to be rational, honest, informative, democratic and clear, is in fact none of these things, but, on the contrary, often illogical, obscure, patronising and one-sided, populated with false analogies, misleading metaphors and impenetrable ambiguities. While such language use is not new, it sounds particularly disturbing when it occurs in the public discourse of democracies, and even more disturbing when, perhaps because of its sheer quantity and familiarity, it passes unchallenged and even unnoticed.

Not all the language associated with GM technology is like this, of course. There are many lucid accounts, which succeed in setting the technical facts before their audience. Many defences begin with a description of just how the process is actually carried out.[2] They recount, for example, how 'genes of interest' can be coated onto very small gold or tungsten pellets one micron in diameter – no bigger, that is, than a speck of dust; how these pellets can be fired at plant tissue on a screen using a .22-calibre cartridge; how the screen disperses the pellets; and how some of them then penetrate the plant tissue, hitting the nuclei of plant cells and allowing the DNA to be wiped off the pellets and incorporated into the plant's chromosome, so that the transformed cell now contains inside it the 'genes of interest'.[3] It is easy to understand why the scientists who write such descriptions think they are persuasive. Changing the genetic make-up of a plant is undoubtedly an extraordinary scientific achievement, and the knowledge involved lends those who do it a degree of authority – even if the process is rather more haphazard than some starry-eyed descriptions would lead us to believe. In addition, it is only natural that the scientists should want to communicate their expertise to others, and that they should view what can and cannot be done in the laboratory as the key factors in the debate.

It is not, however, the details of *how* crops are genetically modified in laboratories which is at issue. The disagreement is rather about *what* crops are modified to do, and the potential effects on humanity and the environment when they are grown commercially on a large scale outside the laboratory. Let us, for the moment, divide these consequences into different types, and list them, more or less according to the prominence they receive. Firstly, there are possible material impacts upon health, biodiversity and food. Secondly, less tangibly, there are social effects – the spread of GM technology can change power relations between nations, and affect how decisions are taken, locally, nationally or internationally. Thirdly, there are ethical issues. For those with a religious faith, GM may disrupt their demarcation between divine and human power, while for non-believers it may also seem an unethical excess of interference in the non-human world. Lastly, there are psychological consequences, changing the way we think about our relation to Nature; and cultural consequences, changing the way that this relation to Nature is used symbolically in recreation, literature and art.

This is a long and varied list. Its range may help to explain the diversity of opinions, the different ways of talking and writing about the same thing, and the failure of commentators even to connect with each other's arguments, let alone agree. As the book progresses I shall try to show how these differences and disagreements are reflected in, even created by, the words chosen to promote them. To do this I need a framework, and the one I shall use is as follows.

In any act of communication there is someone talking, someone being talked to, and something being talked about – providing us with three different focuses for analysis, roughly corresponding to an 'I' (or first person), a 'you' (or second person) and a 'he/she/it/them' (or third person).[4] In talk about GM, the assumption is that genetic modification is what is being talked about (the third person, 'it') and that it is, and should be, at the centre of attention. Speakers present what they say about GM as though their language were indeed a transparent glass, through which they (the 'I' of the discourse) invite their audience (the 'you') to see the truth about GM (the 'it'). In this book, however, the focus is more upon the speakers themselves, and the ways in which, through their choice of words and images, they position the people they are speaking to, trying to make them construct the third-person reality of GM in a particular way – often without their consent.

This book follows this structure of the 'triangle of communication'. In Part I we focus explicitly upon the most powerful speakers. There is a chapter each for politicians, scientists, journalists and businesses, though with an eye to the ways in which they constantly poach from and trespass upon each other. Part II shifts to what is spoken about, showing how arguments which seem to concern matters of fact also always reflect differences of ideology and belief. Finally, in Part III, we turn briefly to the last remaining point of the triangle, the people who are spoken to, and the degree to which they do, or do not, accept the role and viewpoint which have been assigned to them.

The various participants bring to the debate very different perspectives and traditions. They see the issue of GM in diverse ways, as primarily political, scientific, commercial or ethical. Each perspective has its own ways of talking (or 'discourse'), and their coming together can create many misunderstandings. To date, however, the discourse of the debate has received little attention. Yet, as all players increasingly realise, this is a war of words which will be won as much by the presentation of arguments as by action in the laboratory, fields or supermarkets.

In this book the main focus is upon arguments for GM crops and food on the grounds that, as these are the proposals for change, they require more scrutiny than those to preserve the status quo. My purpose is to outline the terrain, tracing both the pathways which connect the different types of argument and the fences which keep them apart, and to analyse the confusion which arises when protagonists shift (inadvertently or deliberately) between perspectives, are unsure of their location, or try to be in two places at once. It is not a technical book for specialists, whether biologists or linguists. (For those unfamiliar with the scientific issues, a summary is given in Appendix 1.) It aims rather to be for the general reader: someone who, though perhaps unfamiliar with the technicalities of language analysis, nevertheless has a generally well-informed interest in developments in language use. For this reason I give, where necessary, some brief explanation of ideas and procedures from linguistics. More often than not, however, the book appeals not to any specialised linguistic insight but simply to a rational scrutiny of what is being said, and why.

However we divide and categorise the world, the GM question resonates in the political and economic relations between the various (overlapping) power centres and cultural blocs: the USA, the Americas, Europe, Africa, the Islamic world, South East Asia, the developing world. Thus, although in 2002, 99 per cent of the world's legally planted GM crops were in only five countries[5] (the USA, Argentina, Canada, China and South Africa), in 2003 there were significant expansions. New regulations were discussed – though delayed – in Brazil,[6] new licences were granted for GM planting in Australia, and the pressure mounted on developing countries to 'go GM' and on Europe to end its moratorium on commercial cultivation. It is in any case in the nature of major agricultural changes to be global. Flora and fauna do not heed political boundaries, and neither does the food market. What happens anywhere is bound to affect us all.

The topic of GM crops and food is thus inherently international, and its development is necessarily world news. Although the texts analysed in this book are predominantly from Britain and the USA, their relevance is by no means limited to these two nations. As the USA is the country with most influence on global agricultural policy, and is itself one of the world's largest food producers, its foregrounding needs no justification. Britain is much smaller and less influential, yet it is a country in which the debate has been particularly heated, with the government pulled, as on many other issues, between its European partners and the USA, while seeking also to exert its influence on world events. This book focuses upon arguments for GM in Britain in particular, not only for the practical reason that Britain is where my research was conducted, but also because, being more divided than other countries, it crystallises the issues in ways which are relevant globally, and shows them to be part of a larger international picture in which GM is one of many interrelated conflicts. While I have been writing, the topic of GM has periodically been driven out of the news by events on the international stage, especially military campaigns and the international reaction to them. But these events and the disagreements over them are not entirely separate from what is discussed here. GM is part of a much larger debate in which themes, issues and ideological differences recur and intertwine. Analysing GM language can help us understand, more generally, the polarisation of opinion and understanding – between individuals, between cultures and between nations – which characterises so much of contemporary life.

Part I

THE SPEAKERS

1

POLITICIANS

'The quality of our lives'

Many public figures have talked about GM. We shall begin at the top, with a president, a prime minister and a prince.

On 16 May 2001, with 'A proclamation by the President of the United States of America', George W. Bush launched a 'National Biotechnology Week'.[1] The proclamation begins with a broad sweep:

> For thousands of years, man has been utilizing and modifying biological processes to improve man's quality of life. Scientific advances have enabled biotechnology to play an increasingly large role in the development of new products that enhance all areas of our lives.

A second paragraph then catalogues recent triumphs in medical biotechnology.

> In the battle against disease, our ever-increasing knowledge of cellular and genetic processes continues to improve the quality of our health care. Biotechnology has contributed to the development of vaccines, antibiotics, and other drugs that have saved or prolonged the lives of millions of people.

In the third paragraph attention is turned to GM agriculture and food.

> Consumers enjoy continual improvements to the quality and quantity of our Nation's food supply. Genetic engineering

9

will enable farmers to modify crops so that they will grow on land that was previously considered infertile. In addition, it will enable farmers to grow produce with enhanced nutritional value. We also are benefiting from crops that resist plant diseases and insects, thus reducing the use of pesticides.

This is condensed, powerful prose. It swiftly introduces the key themes which we shall encounter many times. First is the historical contextualisation. Recent biotechnology is seen as part of humanity's age-old intervention in Nature. Indeed, in the second sentence of the first paragraph, the word 'biotechnology' could seem to refer to *any* utilisation or modification of biological processes, and thus to embrace all types of agriculture and medicine. By this definition, there is nothing essentially new about genetic engineering. It is just the beneficial acceleration of a long-standing traditional process.

Next comes a catalogue of medical advances. (I have not cited these in full, because this book is concerned with medical biotechnology only when, as here, it is coupled with an argument about GM food.) 'Biotechnology' (a comparatively recent word usually used to describe contemporary developments[2]) is projected backwards in time to encompass such obviously beneficial developments as vaccination (an example we shall encounter many times), antibiotics and life-preserving drugs. It is a compelling list – for who could challenge a technology which reduces suffering, ageing and disease? By association, surely, other GM technologies will share some reflected glory. This prepares the way for a summary, in the third paragraph, of the benefits of GM crops themselves. They will increase food production and nutrition, while simultaneously reducing environmental damage. There is even something of the frontier spirit of America here, with farmers able to grow crops 'on land that was considered infertile'.

It all sounds too good and exciting to be true – and perhaps it is. But let us take these claims at face value for the moment, and look at some details of how they are expressed. First, let us consider who Bush means when he uses the words 'we' and 'our' – two little words which, as we shall see throughout this book, are made to work very hard in contemporary public discourse.

In the opening paragraph, Bush seems to be talking unequivocally about humanity as a whole: 'man' (spelled, rather surprisingly, with a small 'm'). So when, at the end of this first paragraph, he refers to 'our lives', we can assume he is talking about all people everywhere. This meaning then carries over, we might assume, to the discussion of medical advances in the second paragraph, although the phrase 'our health care' has a rather more insular ring to it, as though Bush was now talking about the USA, rather than humanity at large or throughout history. The claim that biotechnology has 'prolonged the lives of millions of people', however, seems to return us to the world as a whole.

So there is something equivocal in these opening uses of 'we' and 'our'. Is all humanity included in these terms, or just the population of the USA? By the third paragraph, however, the one directly concerned with GM crops, this ambiguity seems to disappear. 'Consumers enjoy continual improvements to the quality and quantity of our Nation's food supply.' Here, 'our' clearly refers only to the citizens of 'our Nation' (spelled, unlike 'man', with a capital letter). Does this mean – retrospectively, however – that 'our lives' in the first paragraph actually referred to American lives? And when we come to the last sentence of the third paragraph, beginning 'We also are benefiting', is that all humanity again or just Americans? It is not really clear.

The word 'we' of course is inherently and notoriously vague: a way of getting people on your side without being too specific as to who is – and is not – included. I have been using it myself – as you may have noticed – in rather a vague way too, to mean something like 'the readers' when actually, you might argue, I am just asserting my own views, and trying to make you feel part of them. In that sense, George W. Bush is doing nothing unusual. Indeed, ambiguity in the use of this first-person plural pronoun is built into English, and many other languages too. 'We' in English can be used in two quite different ways: to mean either 'all people involved' (the so-called 'inclusive we') or just 'some people involved' (the so-called 'exclusive we'). The difference can be brought out by considering a situation such as the following. Suppose two gangs of youths confront each other, and the leader of one gang shouts, 'We have to run, the police are after us'. By 'we' and 'us' he could be referring to members of both gangs or only to members of his own. Some languages, such as Malay,[3] have distinct words for these two senses: one meaning 'we but not you' and the other meaning 'we and you together'. So in some ways, this ambiguity of 'we' is inevitable, part and parcel of using English. There is a key issue here, nevertheless, which the ambiguity disguises and which needs to be clarified. If there are benefits in GM technology, who precisely are they for?

The shifting meaning of 'we' (humanity, Americans), however, is not the only ambiguity in this proclamation which at first glance seems to be so clear and straightforward. There is also the relation between medical and food biotechnology. Are they the same sort of thing?[4] Are the virtues of medical biotechnology, if real, automatically transferable to GM agriculture, simply because they both come under the heading of biotechnology? That seems to be the implication. But does it follow logically? Medical biotech is presented as fighting 'a battle' (presumably winnable) against ageing and disease. But if GM crops are fighting a battle, who or what is the enemy?

Whatever the implied similarity, there is a marked change in the third paragraph which focuses specifically upon food and crops. The language is now one of commerce rather than philanthropy. The beneficiaries are now 'consumers'; the phrase 'our Nation's food supply' introduces a note of strategic, even military defence planning. Retrospectively, though, perhaps that commercial note was there all along, even in the first paragraph, in the phrase 'new products'. Did people, 'thousands of years' ago, think in such terms?

That opening phrase 'For thousands of years' marks continuity with the past as an important theme. Biotechnology is portrayed not as a radical new departure, but as 'utilizing and modifying biological processes', a definition which would include agriculture and selective breeding even in their earliest forms. Continuity with the past seems to be sought. The whole thrust of the opening paragraphs is to project backwards in time the scope of the word 'biotechnology' so that it includes, and acquires the glory of, the whole history of human achievement. Even the somewhat archaic genre of this statement helps place it in this historical current of continuity. It is called 'A proclamation' and concludes grandly with the formula:

> IN WITNESS WHEREOF, I have hereunto set my hand this sixteenth day of May, in the year of our Lord two thousand one, and of the Independence of the United States of America the two hundred and twenty-fifth.

But before this grand conclusion there are two other paragraphs. Though I will not scrutinise them as closely as the others, they are worth quoting in full. One summarises concisely the case for the environmental benefits of GM technology. The other raises the issue of the relation between the USA and the rest of the world in decision-making about GM:

> The environmental benefits of biotechnology can be realized through the increased ability of manufacturers to produce their products with less energy, pollution, and waste. In addi-

tion, the development of new biotechnology promises to improve our ability to clean up toxic substances from soil and water and improve waste management techniques. Our Nation stands as a global leader in research and development, in large part because of our successes in understanding and utilizing the biological processes of life. The field of biotechnology is important to the quality of our lives, the protection of our environment, and the strength of our economy. We must continue to be leaders in the pursuit of knowledge and technology, and we must be vigilant to ensure that new technologies are regulated and used responsibly towards achieving noble goals.

In terms of the triangle of communication, it is interesting to note how Bush uses language to portray himself, to position his audience, and to present the advent of GM technology. He speaks with all the authority and verbal trappings of his office, and although he does not invite his audience to respond, he magnanimously positions them with himself, by referring to both as 'we', simultaneously members of 'man[kind]' and 'our Nation'. GM is to be seen as the next step forward for both.

This brief proclamation can serve a useful purpose in illustrating and focusing our attention on key themes in the war of words over GM crops:

- Who is GM food technology for? (Who are 'we'?)
- Is it a radical change or just acceleration of traditional manipulation of nature?
- Does it improve health?
- Does it have 'environmental benefits'?
- Who will regulate it and ensure it is used responsibly?

'Overrun by protestors'

All of these key themes appear in a speech made almost exactly one year after Bush's, on 23 May 2002, by British Prime Minister Tony Blair.[5] There is the same alternation between the interests of humanity and of one state, the same appeal to past achievements, the same linking of medical and crop biotechnology, though the positioning of both audience and topic is somewhat different. At 4,700 words, moreover, the speech is much longer than Bush's pithy 483-word proclamation. In addition, it deals with 'British science' as a whole –

although it was only the comments on biotechnology which made the headlines the next day. As the speech is too long to analyse in full, we shall confine ourselves to some passages specifically concerned with GM crops.

Although Blair echoes Bush's claims, he also introduces a new topic, noticeably absent from the presidential proclamation. He refers to opposition to GM technology. Indeed, it was apparently concern about this opposition which motivated the speech in the first place.

> The idea of making this speech has been in my mind for some time. The final prompt for it came, curiously enough, when I was in Bangalore in January. I met a group of academics, who were also in business in the biotech field. They said to me bluntly: Europe has gone soft on science; we are going to leapfrog you and you will miss out. They regarded the debate on GM here and elsewhere in Europe as utterly astonishing. They saw us as completely overrun by protestors and pressure groups who used emotion to drive out reason. And they didn't think we had the political will to stand up for proper science.

That Tony Blair should be preoccupied with opposition to GM, while George W. Bush proceeds as though it did not exist, is hardly surprising. This difference reflects that between Europe, where opposition has been strong, and the USA, where it has had little impact (a foretaste of the different public responses the two leaders were to encounter not long afterwards over the invasion of Iraq). It also reflects differences between the two types of communication. Blair is making a long speech; Bush is issuing a brief proclamation. Nevertheless, there is something noteworthy about the manner in which Blair presents the topic. He introduces it not by stating his own view, but by quoting somebody else's: 'a group of academics, who were also in business in the biotech field' from Bangalore. Theirs is a tough, honest and presumably well-informed voice which speaks 'bluntly', saying: 'we are going to leapfrog you, and you will miss out'.

This raises many questions. We might wonder why Tony Blair has selected these particular voices from all those he must have heard on his travels both inside and outside Europe. We might ask why the opinions of this 'group of academics' in Bangalore should influence British policy. More factually, as a lawyer would (and Blair, incidentally, is trained as a barrister), we might ask what *exactly* they did say? Is Blair quoting them word for word as he seems to be ('Europe has gone soft on science . . .') or just paraphrasing? As he is referring to more than one person, he cannot be quoting them verbatim unless they all spoke in unison. Is this perhaps why there are no quotation marks in the written version? And most probingly of all, we might ask exactly who these people were. What exactly are their academic and business credentials? It is not clear from the phrase 'in Bangalore' whether these people are themselves from Bangalore (a city in southern India) or were simply visiting, as Tony Blair himself was.[6] If the latter, it seems important to the argument to know where they were from.

These questions provide an insight into why quoting someone else in an argument is a very clever and often successful rhetorical strategy. It allows the speaker to borrow the opinion and the authority of the people quoted (as academics, they know their science; as business people, they know their economics; if they are Indians, they are familiar with poverty), while simultaneously remaining independent and detached. It gives room for retreat. This view is simultaneously Blair's and not Blair's. And if it is challenged, he can disown it.

Even if the reported words are taken at face value, however, a good deal remains unclear. Does the pronoun 'we' (when they say 'we are going to leapfrog you') refer just to this group of people, to India, to Asia or to the whole world outside Europe? Does 'you' mean Britain or Europe? And are Europeans, if that is who 'you' refers to, going to be overtaken in scientific understanding or in economic prosperity? And how are we to take the words Tony Blair reports? Are they a threat or a taunt, a friendly warning or a call for change? Most importantly, does he share their view or is he just reporting it?

Like the Bush proclamation, this paragraph raises the issue of who is meant by the words 'we' and 'us'. 'They saw us', Blair says, 'as completely overrun by protestors and pressure groups who used emotion to drive out reason.' Rather oddly, this wording suggests that these 'protestors and pressure groups' are somehow outsiders rather than Europeans themselves. 'Us' must mean 'Europeans other than the protestors and pressure groups' – unless people can be overrun by themselves.

An interesting insight into the nature of this phrase 'overrun by' can be provided by computerised corpus analysis. In this comparatively recent technique of linguistic analysis, data banks (or 'corpora', the plural of 'corpus') are assembled containing millions of words of actual texts and transcriptions. These can then be searched very rapidly to yield extensive information about word use which would not have been revealed by intuition.[7] We can discover which words are used most frequently, and the combinations which they typically form with others. (Frequent co-occurrences of words are called 'collocations'.) One particularly revealing product of such analysis is a 'concordance', giving us a word or phrase down the centre of the screen, and the context in which it occurred to either side, as follows:[8]

```
                Here, in a pop-town still overrun by middle-aged wrinklies in beards
       Range', with its vision of Europe overrun by jackboots is only effective if
       ancients when the Roman Empire was overrun by Nordic barbarians destroying
       on their belts, in case they get overrun by a fire. The device, an aluminum
  outskirts of Srinagar was literally overrun by mourners. The crowd which
  into the jungle after their camp was overrun by Tamil Tiger guerillas at the
  of the camp (at Mankulam), which was overrun by Tamil Tiger rebels at the
            regime which was rapidly being overrun by the new liberalism, and the new
     safe area' of Srebrenica from being overrun by the Serbs in July, Yasushi
          to Croatian control after being overrun by Serb forces in 1991. [p] The
       order into a country that has been overrun by bandits, black [p] marketeers
  well as fun. If the thought of being overrun by family and friends is already
              the Himalayas and high Andes are overrun by tourists, travel agents quick-
       Rambouillet and Chambord, are now overrun by rabbits, pheasants, hares, boar
              the UN-designated safe haven overrun by Bosnian Serbs last summer,
             occupied by the Serbs which was overrun by Muslim/Croat Federation troops
       recently offered an old farmhouse overrun by creepers which, the details
       the oil-rich Kuwait is from being overrun by the tyrant Saddam Hussein four
  Crimean peninsula before they were overrun by the Soviets. And finally, it
     on August 2, 1990, Kuwait had been overrun by an Iraqi juggernaut seemingly
       Hulegu Khan and again by Tamerlane, overrun by Turks and Persians, Ottomans
            Zinc, and Platinum in the north, overrun by the Royal Scots Dragoon Guards,
  unconfirmed reports that it had been overrun by Iraqi troops are not true. Jean
            the US mission in Kuwait had been overrun by Iraqi troops. Jean Cochran,
     a school. The city's cemetery was overrun by Georgian forces that same
     For the past four years, it's been overrun by tourists and reporters and
       targeted for relief have now been overrun by Serbian forces, thousands of
```

Here we can see that 'overrun by' collocates with words referring to military forces, with enemies or potential enemies of Britain ('Nordic barbarians', 'Iraqi troops', 'Bosnian Serbs', 'Soviets'), with pests ('rabbits', 'creepers') or more generally with anyone or anything seen in a particular context as unwanted (here 'tourists', 'fire', 'middle-aged wrinklies'). It seems reasonable to conclude that Tony Blair, by using this phrase to describe protestors, flavours them with this quality too. When a word frequently occurs in negative descriptions in this way, it is described by corpus linguists as having a negative 'semantic prosody',[9] – a term that we shall use again.

Blair's Bangalori advisers, moreover, characterise these opponents as people governed by 'emotion' rather than 'reason'. With unconscious irony, however, Blair summarises this view in a sentence which (with its alliterative 'protestors and pressure groups' and its hyperbolic 'completely overrun') seems itself to be based on emotion rather than reason.

As the speech moves on, the characterisation of opposition to GM technology as emotional rather than reasonable reveals itself as Tony Blair's too, though he is less brusque in his dismissal of opposition than is the 'group of academics' in Bangalore.

> So Britain can benefit enormously from scientific advance. But precisely because the advances are so immense, people worry. And, of course, many of these worries are entirely serious. In GM crops, I can find no serious evidence of health risks. But there are genuine and real concerns over biodiversity and gene transfer. Human cloning raises legitimate moral questions. Advances in arms technology makes the world less safe. Humanity has, for the first time, the capacity for vast prosperity or to destroy itself completely.

Again there is unconscious irony. For a passage extolling reason over emotion, the reasoning seems oddly flawed. There are so many points which are simply omitted. Altogether, Blair mentions four sources of concern: health risks, possible damage to biodiversity, gene transfer and morality. He tells us that he can find 'no serious evidence of health risks'. But he does *not* say he can find no serious evidence of gene transfer or damage to biodiversity. Though this seems to be implied, it is not stated directly, although it should be for the rebuttal to be systematic and complete. And what does he mean by '*serious* evidence'? Is there some other kind of evidence which, for reasons not given, he does not consider serious? On the subject of morality, he mentions 'legitimate moral questions', but only in relation to human cloning. Does that imply that human cloning is the only biotechnology activity which raises moral questions? And if there are '*legitimate* moral questions' about human cloning, are there also some kind of illegitimate moral questions which people are asking about other matters? Then, out of the blue, he mentions 'arms technology'. But the *logical* connection between worry about arms build-ups and worry about GM food is not clear. Given the preoccupations of Western governments at the time, this shift of topic seems to link the GM issue to that of 'rogue states' and the 'axis of evil': North Korea, Iraq and Iran.[10]

A key word, here and in Blair's rhetoric more generally, is 'people'.[11] Like 'we', it is a generic term which is rather unclear. Does it mean 'all people' or just 'some people'? Here, by inference, it seems to mean uninformed people, who, like the Europeans described by the Bangalore academics, are governed by emotion rather than reason. Their opposition stems from 'worry' rather than 'serious evidence'. It arises from opposition to technology in general, rather than any specific or reasoned objection. This view is amplified in the next paragraph too.

> People have an understandable concern about the pace of change, about the new and the unknown. They are concerned that technology dehumanises society. They are concerned by their belief that scientists contradict each other, or can be unreliable. And about what they see as the inability of government to regulate science properly.

There is certainly more apparent sympathy here than there was in the words of the Bangalori academics. Blair sees 'understandable concern'. Yet the phrasing ('*their belief that* scientists contradict each other', '*what they see as* the inability of government') strongly suggests that, however 'understandable', these concerns are unjustified. It does not concede that scientists do actually contradict each other, or that government is ever unable to regulate science. They are dismissed as an irrational reaction to the 'pace of change'.

But the condemnation of opposition gradually gets stronger. In the next paragraph, opponents have become, by association, not just worriers, but ignorant and destructive opponents of progress.

> In some cases, these concerns descend into a fear, which is amplified by parts of the media. Some of these concerns are not new. You don't need to go back to Galileo for examples. Lightning conductors, invented by Benjamin Franklin, were initially torn down, even from churches, because it was believed they thwarted God's will. There were riots in the streets when the smallpox vaccine was introduced. Smallpox has now been eliminated. In the early days of heart transplants they were attacked as unnatural or dehumanising, but

in surveys today heart transplants are seen as one of the most beneficial results of modern science.

Here, as Bush did, Blair places biotechnology in a historical context, seeing it as a continuation of human progress, linking it in this case with a string of scientific discoveries, including two of incontrovertible benefit to humanity: lightning conductors and the smallpox vaccine. This is argument by loose association. GM technology is the same kind of thing because it is a new discovery, so opposition to it must also be the same. 'Fear' of GM crops must be irrational, founded on religious dogma, like opposition to Galileo or Franklin.

Blair shares with Bush an unqualified support for GM. Yet in terms of the communicative triangle, he goes about promoting it in a rather different way. Blair's 'it' is not so much GM itself as different reactions to it. Rather than embracing everyone in a single general category, his words – and in particular his use of pronouns and generic referents – divide people into different categories. On the one hand, there are rational, progressive, well-informed and 'serious' thinkers like himself; on the other, there are 'protestors'. Torn between the two are 'people' who worry, understandably but wrongly, and do not know which way to turn. The thrust of the speech is to invite this last category, under Blair's guidance, to choose the side of sense, to become part of the 'we'. This leaves the protestors ('them') as people to talk about but not to talk to. In doing this Blair presents a particular vision of those who resist GM crop technology – as mindless 'Luddites' whipped up by the press – which denies the possibility that there might also be rational and informed opposition, with views based upon considered reflection.

'Bees and the wind'

By way of an illuminating comparison, let us look now, equally critically, at an opposing view. It is perhaps the most famous statement of opposition to GM: an article by Prince Charles in the *Daily Mail* of Tuesday, 1 June 1999. The first part of this article[12] reads as follows. (GMO stands for genetically modified organism.)

> At the end of last year I set up a discussion forum on my website on the question of GMOs. I wanted to encourage wider public debate about what I see as a fundamental issue and one which affects each and every one of us, and future generations.

There was a huge response – some 10,000 replies have indicated that public concern about the use of GM technology has been growing. Many food producers and retailers have clearly felt the same overwhelming anxiety from their consumers who are demanding a choice in what they eat. A number of them have now banned GM ingredients from their own-brand products.

But the debate continues to rage. Not a day goes by without some new piece of research claiming to demonstrate either the safety or the risks of GM technology. It is very hard for people to know just who is right. Few of us are able to interpret all the scientific information which is available – and even the experts don't always agree. But what I believe the public's reaction shows is that instinctively we are nervous about tampering with Nature when we can't be sure that we know enough about all the consequences.

Having followed this debate very closely for some while now, I believe that there are still a number of unanswered questions that need to be asked.

1. Do we need GM food in this country?
On the basis of what we have seen so far, we don't appear to need it at all. The benefits, such as there are, seem to be limited to the people who own the technology and the people who farm on an industrialised scale. We are constantly told that this technology may have huge benefits for the future. Well, perhaps. But we have all heard claims like that before and they don't always come true in the long run – look at the case of antibiotic growth promoters in animal feedstuff . . .

2. Is GM food safe for us to eat?
There is certainly no evidence to the contrary. But how much evidence do we have? And are we looking at the right things? The major decisions about what can be grown and can be sold are taken on the basis of studying what is known about the original plant, comparing it to the genetically modified variety, and then deciding whether the two are 'substantially equivalent'. But is it enough to look only at what is already known? Isn't there at least a possibility that the new crop (particularly those that have been made resistant to antibiotics) will behave in unexpected ways, producing toxic or

allergic reactions? Only independent scientific research, over a long period, can provide the final answer.

3. Why are the rules for approving GM foods so much less stringent than those for new medicines produced using the same technology?
Before drugs are released into the marketplace they have to undergo the most rigorous testing – and quite right too. But GM food is also designed in a laboratory for human consumption, albeit in different circumstances. Surely, it is equally important that we are confident that they will do us no harm?

4. How much do we really know about the environmental consequences of GM crops?
Laboratory tests showing that pollen from GM maize in the United States caused damage to the caterpillars of Monarch butterflies provide the latest cause for concern. If GM crops can do this to butterflies, what damage might they cause to other species? But more alarmingly perhaps, this GM maize is not under test. It is already being grown commercially throughout large areas of the United States of America.

Surely this effect should have been discovered by the company producing the seeds, or the regulatory authorities who approved them for sale, at a much earlier stage? Indeed, how much more are we going to learn the hard way about the impact of GM crops on the environment?

Linguistically, there is something very striking about this article by Prince Charles. It is composed almost entirely of interrogative sentences. Indeed, of the seventy-one sentences which make up the entire article, twenty-seven – more than one-third – end in a question mark. This is an unusual rhetorical strategy, and, faced by all these royal wonderings, one cannot help asking in reply at least two questions of one's own: why did the Prince decide to adopt this style and what effect might it have on his readers?

The answer perhaps lies in the fact that he is a prince. There is a danger that he will be perceived as arrogant or interfering from on high. He must not appear to be ordering people around or asserting his own view in a way which forbids any contradiction. Royal questions will go down better than royal commands. The interrogative style is the perfect antidote to arrogance. But why? Why should interrogative sentences seem less arrogant? This is an instance where some linguistic analysis can certainly be of help.

Interrogatives ending in question marks (such as 'Do we need GM food in this country?') are one of three types of sentences. The others are declaratives ending in a full stop ('We don't need GM food in this country.') and imperatives often ending in an exclamation mark ('Stop GM food in this country!'). We usually equate them with, and even loosely refer to them as, questions, statements and orders. But these are what linguists call functional labels, telling us what the sentences are doing rather than just telling us about their grammatical form; the correspondence between linguistic form and function is by no means straightforward. An interrogative can function as a statement ('Do I feel awful?') or an exclamation ('How wicked is that?') or even an order ('Have you cleaned your teeth yet?').

Indeed, many of the interrogatives in this article are clearly only questions in the rhetorical sense. Sometimes they function only as a prelude to an answer. 'Do we need GM food . . .? . . . we don't appear to need it at all.' Sometimes they contain a hidden assertion, known technically as a 'presupposition'. For example, the interrogative 'Why are the rules for approving GM foods so much less stringent than those for new medicines produced using the same technology?' takes it as given that GM legislation is actually less stringent than medical legislation. In addition, although there appear to be two or more voices, they are in reality all the Prince's. He is both witness and cross-examiner, interrogated and interrogator. It is his catechism throughout.

An interesting insight into the effect of interrogatives is provided by research into conversational differences between men and women. In the early days of such research, it was claimed[13] that women are more likely to use interrogatives in conversation than men, inviting agreement with their point of view rather than stating it baldly as their own, and saying things like 'Do you think there might be another way of doing it?' rather than 'I think we should do it differently.'

Once, when I told a class of undergraduates about this research, a female undergraduate challenged it by saying, to the amusement of her classmates, 'But surely that can't be true, can it?' Although she got herself into a tangle, she was probably right. The finding has been disputed, and it is certainly oversimplified. Understandably, many people remain unconvinced by such a quantitative approach to differences in conversational behaviour.[14] What is relevant to us here is not the facts of this research, but rather the assumptions about the effect of interrogatives, whoever uses them. Those feminist linguists who made the quantitative claim saw the interrogative as encouraging compromise and agreement, and thus regarded its apparently more frequent use by women as evidence that they are less assertive and more collaborative than men. So whether or not it is actually more typical of females, it is certainly associated with both feminine and feminist virtues: tolerance, dialogue, willingness to listen and to negotiate. The point is that questioning is seen as less combative, less *macho* than constant declaratives.

So, given the bad press which goes with being a prince, it is perhaps a good tactic to use. It dispels any aftertaste of arrogance which might be imputed to him by republicans and democrats or anyone with a distrust of wealth and privilege.

This mild tone is not immediately evident, however. In contrast with what follows, the opening paragraph has a rather more imperious tone, with first-person pronouns declaring the Prince's opinions, desires and actions.

> At the end of last year *I set up a discussion forum* on my website on the question of GMOs. *I wanted to encourage wider public debate* about *what I see as a fundamental issue* and one which affects each and every one of us, and future generations [my emphasis].

It is as though the whole debate and the public response to it were of his making. Yet even here, the virtue of dialogue is heavily implied, and, despite the assertive tone, what he is instigating is, after all, a 'discussion forum' and 'a public debate'. And by the third sentence, any arrogance in the opening has evaporated, with the authority appearing to pass from the Prince himself to other people: 'There was a huge response – some 10,000 replies have indicated that public concern about the use of GM technology has been growing.'

Thus these '10,000 replies' are given as the driving force behind the article, and, rather than stating his own view, Charles seems merely to be dutifully relaying those of others. As Tony Blair did, he presents himself initially as listening and repeating rather than asserting his own view.

Many other voices are cited throughout Charles's article, including retailers, researchers, governments, charities, farmers. But it is not only the constant citation of others which gives this article its demo-cratic, reasonable tone. There are colloquial conversation phrases, as though the Prince were actually talking to the reader: 'Well, perhaps',

'– and quite right too', 'Not a day goes by'. It is like a conversation. And he is careful to talk of 'we', as though this was a shared problem, rather than 'you': 'we are nervous', 'we can't be sure that we know enough'. Yet, as in the Bush proclamation and the Blair speech, it is interesting to reflect on exactly who is included in the scope of 'we'. Like theirs, it is not as all-inclusive as it might seem. This is clear, for example, in the sentence 'We are constantly told that this technology may have huge benefits for the future', where 'we' clearly excludes the people who are advocating GM. Elsewhere, there are further clues that his use of 'we' does not include scientists, producers, retailers, legislators and 'the people who own the technology and the people who farm on an industrialised scale'. 'We', in other words, for Charles, seems to mean something like 'people who have neither expertise nor a vested interest in GM technology', a category in which he does, however, seem to include himself. Thus through the use of this pronoun he divides society into two groups, categorising himself, perhaps rather controversially, as one of the ordinary people.

Though the views are very different, in terms of the communicative triangle the effects are not dissimilar to Blair's speech. The interrogative structures and conversational syntax position the readers as participants in a conversation with Charles, and then invite them to look with him both at the effects of GM and at the people, those not included in the conversation, who are promulgating it.

Same views, different voices

Running through everything we have looked at so far are the two related themes of authority and dialogue. Are there certain voices – of scientists, politicians, past generations, the 'people', the poor – which should have more say in this debate than others? Or should decisions and some kind of consensus emerge from dialogue? And if so, should all voices be listened to, or are some beyond the pale?

In Bush's 'proclamation' he speaks (appropriately enough for the genre) with a single voice and with confident authority. Blair and Charles, however, as we have seen, constantly invoke the voices of other people to back up what they are saying. For Blair, it is the voice of scientific evidence over the voices of those 'people' who 'worry'. For Charles, it is the other way round: the 10,000 people who contacted his web page seem to carry, by their very number and the spontaneity and strength of their concern, a kind of 'honest John' authority suggesting that both scientists and government should think again. A voice which both seem to invoke is that of those suffering from poverty and malnutrition: those whose authority stems from their need. Charles, who does this rather more explicitly than Blair, cites – in parts of the article not quoted here (see Appendix 2) – the opinions of Christian Aid and 'representatives of 20 African states including Ethiopia'. Blair seems to invoke – albeit ambiguously – the authority of voices from Bangalore. All these carry particular moral authority by virtue of their involvement with the people on whom GM may have the greatest impact.

We have here then two very different styles of argument, cutting across the more obvious distinction between proponents and opponents. On the one hand is Bush, speaking with a strong and confident single voice of his own, not attributing views to anyone other than himself. On the other are Blair and Charles who, despite their very evident differences of opinion over GM, share a rhetorical technique: they argue by invoking the words and opinions of others – scientists (both living and dead), farmers, religious leaders and just the very vaguely defined 'people'.

These two styles of argument represent two fundamentally opposed kinds of discourse. In one, referred to by the Russian thinker Bakhtin as 'monologic', there is one clear authoritative voice; in the other, referred to as 'dialogic' or 'heteroglossic', there are two or many voices, growing over and around each other in ways which can make it hard to disentangle exactly which view is attributable to whom,[15] and thus to be sure what the speaker who cites, invokes or animates them[16] actually thinks. In some cases (though not those of either Blair or Charles) it may even appear that the speaker has no firm personal view other than that which is the sum of all the others. Literary texts are particularly noted for their capacity to contain many points of view at once without committing themselves to any one.[17]

But how are we to judge these two styles of speaking? On the face of it, it might seem that monologic discourse is authoritarian while heteroglossic argument is more democratic, more willing to seek consensus. Yet this is not necessarily the case. Citation of authorities, rather than observed evidence or the speaker's own view, can also be oppressive. Moreover, the speaker who constantly incorporates the voices of others necessarily both selects and colours what they say, and the words remain, even when attributed to others, in an important sense the speaker's own, despite an illusion to the contrary. Unhedged, direct speaking has at least the virtue of straightforwardness even when we disagree with it. For this reason, the expressions 'straight talk' and 'direct speaking' both have positive connotations, and understandably have considerable appeal.

This intertwining of viewpoints can be evident at every level of language from the briefest sentence to whole texts. It can even happen within the space of a single word, as when a speaker, for humorous effect, chooses to imitate someone else's pronunciation, or when in writing we put inverted commas around a word to indicate it is not our own. At sentence level this merging of voices happens in a variety of ways. It may be extremely vague, allowing the force of a claim (which is nevertheless still being made) to be somehow softened by being attributed to unspecified others. Imagine, for example, a newspaper saying:

> It is widely believed that, if appropriately developed, GM crops could be used deliberately to improve the environment.

An alternative might be to attribute the views to some large but still very general group, as in:

> Scientists say that, if appropriately developed, GM crops could be used deliberately to improve the environment.

Or a particular named individual could be quoted:

> Robert says that, if appropriately developed, GM crops could be used deliberately to improve the environment.

In the last case, different ways of naming the same speaker can also introduce new voices, so that Robert's opinion may be perceived rather differently if we refer to him not only by his first name, but with his title and office:[18]

> Lord May said that, if appropriately developed, GM crops could be used deliberately to improve the environment.

> Lord May, the President of the Royal Society, has said that if appropriately developed, GM crops could be used deliberately to improve the environment.

In this last case his view carries within it the endorsement of the British establishment and its most august scientific society. In all of these cases, the speaker draws attention to a point of view, but also maintains some distance from it. It is even possible to cite a view and reject it in the same sentence:

> Scientists have wrongly claimed that, if appropriately developed, GM crops could be used deliberately to improve the environment.

There are very many ways in which different voices can be incorporated into what is being said, and the mixture (as we have seen in Tony Blair's reference to the people he met in Bangalore) can be dense and difficult to disentangle, leaving us wondering whether there is any solid ground beneath. As in other public disputes, in the GM debate, with its frequent references to research findings and public announcements, this reporting of the words of others, and the precise attribution of claims to sources, take on a particular importance.

Even when keeping to verbatim quotation, it is possible to colour what is said through the choice of the reporting verb: 'claimed', 'denied', 'announced', 'asserted', 'bragged', 'demonstrated', 'argued', etc. All such verbs (with the possible exceptions of 'said' or 'wrote') both report and judge simultaneously. The effect is different, moreover, when the quotation precedes the reporting clause (a common device in newspapers), rather than following it:

> 'GM crops can only be grown if they get consent', he added.
> (*Daily Mail*, 17 October 2003)

Contrast:

> He added: 'The trials showing that GM maize was better for the environment were invalid.'
> (*Daily Mail*, 17 October 2003)

In the first construction, the voice of the person quoted is foregrounded, that of the reporter left in the background. It is as though the source speaks for itself, and the implication is that its views are correct. In the second the opposite is the case: a sense of distance is created between the reporter's own view and the one quoted. This is even clearer perhaps when the words are paraphrased rather than quoted, and only attributed in the latter part of the sentence:

> GM farming would pollute the countryside for generations,
> the Government's own research revealed yesterday.
>
> (*Daily Mail*, 14 October 2003)

Necessarily, of course, especially in the reporting of scientific or legal documents, words often have to be simplified or summarised, but this is best done as accurately and neutrally as possible. Apparently, the most straightforward way to present the views of another person is to quote them verbatim with a simple preceding reporting verb ('said' or 'wrote') followed by a quotation marked off clearly by inverted commas or indentation. Yet even this can alter the force or meaning of the original, by selecting which words to quote and by recontextualising what was said. This happens, for example, when a casual email between friends or close colleagues suddenly becomes the subject of intense legal and public scrutiny. Even though it is quoted with absolute accuracy, it gains, by crossing the boundary from one context to another or from one type of discourse to another, quite different resonances and significance.[19]

Once the original words cease to be quoted verbatim, however, and are conveyed in some kind of 'reporting clause' ('He said that *x*' rather than 'He said, "*x*"') certainty about what was said diminishes dramatically. This can be shown by a simple and innocuous example. Suppose that I tell you on a Friday what John told me on Monday: 'He said that he might come tomorrow.'

I could quite legitimately be reporting any of the following original words of John's: 'I may come tomorrow.' 'I might come tomorrow.' 'I may come on Tuesday.' 'I might come on Tuesday.' 'I may come on Saturday.' 'I might come on Saturday.'

In ordinary conversation there is nothing sinister about such ambiguity. It is an effect partly of the mechanical tense changes in English when a verb moves from a quoted to a reported clause ('may' changes to 'might' in many people's English), and partly of the fact that a so-called 'deictic' word like 'tomorrow' or 'here' (which identifies something relative to the time and place of speaking rather than in absolute terms) changes its meaning when it is transferred to another time or place. In ordinary conversation, however, any important ambiguities are met with requests for clarification and soon cleared up: 'Did he say he may come or he might come?', 'Do you mean tomorrow, Tuesday, or tomorrow, Saturday?' Moreover, in ordinary conversation based upon mutual trust and cooperation, the precise wording is not likely to be considered important. If I had actually used this sentence to you, I would most likely not have been quoting at all, but merely paraphrasing. I would in any case be unlikely to remember the exact words. But unless you suspect me of setting out to manipulate or deceive, this would not be particularly significant.

In public discourse characterised by distrust and contestation, however, the situation can be very different, and we must be careful of contexts where these ambiguities are courted by the speaker, and there is no reciprocal communication allowing for clarification. We cannot know from secondary sources (such as the following reports in the *Daily Mail*, 17 October 2003) the exact words which were spoken:

> After extensive farm trials, Environment Minister Elliot Morley indicated that genetically-modified oilseed rape and beet would never be approved.
>
> He also questioned whether there would ever be a market for British-grown biotech food because of public opposition.

The same is true of Blair's way of reporting the words of others: 'They said to me bluntly', 'They saw us as completely overrun'.

In these three initial analyses we have already encountered not only key themes but also something of the kind of language use to which GM gives rise. The meanings of words are shifting and vague; they make loose associations; they pose as chatty and relaxed when they are carefully designed. Distinctions between fact and opinion are fudged. Examples seem to be selected to suit the speaker's purpose. It is not even always clear whose the words are, or who is speaking to or about whom.

Perhaps, you might argue, such uses are only to be expected in the polemical discourse of politics and the media. These are not speakers from the domain of science, where language use aspires to be clear, unambiguous, factual and unbiased. It is to the use of language by scientists that we turn in the next chapter.

2

SCIENTISTS

Like plants, arguments come in all shapes and sizes. Some grow separately, some wind around each other. There is a tendency in the GM debate, however, for the propagators of the various points of view to grow a particular species in isolation, separated from its neighbours and kept behind a carefully guarded fence. This isolationism is not confined to any particular perspective. It may be scientific, social, political or ethical. But it is exclusively scientific arguments, assessing what is known about the possible physical consequences of GM as though these were the only relevant factors, which tend to dominate a good deal of the discourse of both opponents and proponents. In time, we shall need to consider whether such arguments can or should be kept separate from those other species of argument about non-physical consequences of GM – political, ethical, economic and aesthetic – which tend to grow in among them, like weeds, from some scientists' points of view.

The previous chapter has shown how three leading public figures – George W. Bush, Tony Blair and Prince Charles – all appeal to science and attempt to recruit its findings to their point of view. But what are the opinions of scientists themselves on the role of scientific evidence in decision-making, and in what kind of language do they express it? How do they account for public reactions to GM, and for the views of opponents? To examine these questions, I intend to do two things: first to examine in detail part of a public statement by a leading member of the scientific community; and second to draw upon the findings of a research project which interviewed GM scientists about exactly these questions.

In asking these questions, however, I am accepting certain categories, which are perhaps not as straightforward as is usually assumed.

My questions presuppose, first, that there is a clear distinction between 'scientists' and 'non-scientists', second that the former are a 'community' who speak with one voice and have 'leading members', third that the categories 'scientists', 'public' and 'opponents' do not overlap. All these assumptions have their problems, as we shall see, but for the moment let us take them at face value, and turn to an address by Lord May, the President of the Royal Society, as an example of a statement by a 'leading member of the scientific community'.[1]

Choosing between fundamentalism and the Enlightenment

A good deal of the speech is devoted to the distinction between science and non-science, apparently stressing the need for science to be rational, evidence-based, provisional and disinterested. What I intend to do is to take extracts and subject them to analysis, as with the texts in Chapter 1. As there may be valid objections to this technique, it is worth saying something in its defence before we begin. (We have used it already on George W. Bush, Tony Blair and Prince Charles, but it may seem that they are somehow fairer game than scientists.)

First, although this was delivered as a speech, it was prepared and was also published as a written document, with all the attendant paraphernalia of section headings, footnotes and references. Consequently, like Blair's 'speech' and Bush's 'proclamation', it has been constructed with all the care which is usually reserved for writing. This makes it legitimate to subject it to a forensic examination of a kind not always justified in the analysis of spontaneous unprepared speech, where people are likely, in the heat of the moment, to say things which they would have expressed differently upon reflection.

Second, as with Tony Blair's speech, we shall necessarily be focusing upon an extract in order to subject it to the kind of careful, rational, evidence-based analysis for which it is itself a plea. Yet in order to come to grips with not only what is being said but how, and the relation between the two (the fundamental aim of this book), it is necessary to say far more *about* each sentence than the sentence says itself. As the whole speech is 9,404 words long, it would be quite impossible to deal with it all. Yet extraction, though necessary, is also unjust,[2] as I am of course choosing a passage which suits my purposes, and which exemplifies what I want to say. As we shall see later in this chapter, there are other kinds of analysis which do allow us to make statements about overall patterns of language use and argumentation.

In one section of the speech, May contrasts the values of the Enlightenment – the change of intellectual climate which made modern science possible – with an opposite approach which he describes as 'Fundamentalism':

The Enlightenment and the many faces of Fundamentalism
Underlying everything I have written here is the assumption that the reader shares the values of the Enlightenment: rational, humane, questioning. These are the values that gave birth to the Royal Society and its motto.[3] When difficult decisions have to be made, we first establish the facts and acknowledge the uncertainties, and then reason together about the choices. I believe these values permeate not only science, medicine and engineering, but also essentially all activity in the arts and humanities, as well as the mainstream expression of many of the great religions.

In contrast are Fundamentalist belief systems. These are found in both West and East, and come in a wide variety of forms, of varying virulence. Their essence is authoritarian, seeking to suppress questioning. Canonical texts, dogma, ideology or revelation – not experiment – are the tools for resolving disputes.

The clash between such closed Fundamentalist belief systems, and the open and questioning mindset of the Enlightenment is found on matters great and small, both within countries and within civilisations as much as among them. Baruma and Margalit have recently analysed this dichotomy under several headings. For science, most Fundamentalists unite in the belief that 'truth' cannot be reliably established by subjecting hypotheses to soulless experimental tests. Rather we should trust, if revelation is not available, to instinct. A clear expression of this view comes from Hitler, ranting against the 'absurdities' of free-thinking scientific research, because 'it leads away from instinct'. Similar views underpinned Mao's Great Leap Forward.

The Taliban, with their heavy curtailment of access to new technology and denial of access to education for women, provide an extreme example of these phenomena. But other forms of Fundamentalism still march, albeit much less dramatically, in the West. They show in quarrels about the teaching of biblically literal Creationism as a valid alternative to evolution in

science courses in schools, and in a kind of Fundamentalism
that wistfully looks to a throw-back world in which nineteenth
century agricultural practices can feed today's burgeoning
population and unproven alternative medicines can afford
the same protection as the products of the pharmaceutical
industry.

To me it seems that there are sleights of hand in this passage which
contradict in practice what is being championed in principle. In the
first paragraph we are told of 'the values of the Enlightenment' –
'rational, humane, questioning' – and how these characterise not
only 'science, medicine and engineering' but also 'the arts and humanities' and 'the mainstream expression of many of the great religions'.
In the next paragraph, this Enlightenment approach is contrasted with
'Fundamentalist belief systems' based upon '[c]anonical texts, dogma,
ideology or revelation – not experiment'. But does this attempt to
bracket 'the great religions' and the sciences together make sense, or
is it just an attempt to create allies by not offending sensibilities?
Which religions are not based upon canonical texts, dogma (in the
non-pejorative sense) and revelation? Are there any religions which
are based upon experiment? The phrasing of the reference to religion,
moreover, is extremely vague. 'Many of the great religions' does not
mean 'all the great religions'. 'Mainstream expression' is similarly
unclear. So we are left wondering precisely which religions and
which 'expressions' are excluded from May's approval. Similar points
might be made about the 'arts and humanities'. Is 'all activity' (my
emphasis) within them really based upon Enlightenment principles?
Was there no art before the Enlightenment?

But by far the most extraordinary aspect of the 'reasoning' in this
extract is its implicit suggestion that all types of fundamentalism
inherit the qualities of all others. Thus the list progresses from Hitler
to Mao to the Taliban to creationist Christians to believers in alternative medicine to people who favour traditional farming methods. This
is argument by analogy, in which one shared feature (acting on a-priori
rather than evidence-based belief) is used to link peaceful advocacy
with violent imposition. There is no necessary connection between
holding beliefs which are based upon 'revelation – not experiment'
and imposing them upon other people. The effect would be very
different if the examples of such beliefs had included those of, say,
Buddha and Jesus. This is argument by selective example, rather like
Blair's list of beneficial technologies.

The choice of examples, moreover, creates a link between opponents of GM within Britain and outsiders and enemies of the British
nation, such as Hitler, Mao and the Taliban. This association is one
which, as we shall see in later chapters, is very salient in arguments
for GM. Here we need to consider not only the literal meanings –
or 'denotations' – of words but also their looser associations and
emotional resonances – or 'connotations'. Thus the style and vocabu-
lary of the initial description of 'fundamentalist belief systems' sounds
rather like someone describing a disease: 'These are found in both
West and East, and come in a wide variety of forms, of varying
virulence.'

Automatic corpus analysis[4] shows the word 'virulence' to collocate
frequently with diseases or objectionable ideas, and to have a markedly
negative prosody. In addition, the choice of the word 'fundamentalism', in the political climate of 2002, was a highly loaded one,
carrying with it connotations outweighing May's definition. It suggests, like the mention of the Taliban, anti-Western fanatics prepared
to resort to violence and terror to achieve their ends. The most
common collocate of 'fundamentalism' in Western media discourse
at this time was 'Islamic'. Is this perhaps the unenlightened 'expression'
of a 'great religion' to which he was referring before? It is hard to
believe that May's choice of word was disingenuous or that he was
unaware of the weight these associations would carry. Emotive
words like this one are not interpreted only as their denotative meaning. Indeed, if we were to stick only to May's literal definition of
'fundamentalism' as 'ideas based upon *a priori* beliefs', we would
have to acknowledge the philosophical truism that all belief systems
must take some such belief as their starting point. In the case of science
these include beliefs in the existence of the material world, the relia-
bility of human perception of that world, and the truth of rational
inductive reasoning. The fact that most people (including me) share
these beliefs does not negate their a-priori nature. But this is not
what May means by 'fundamentalism'.

In another part of the speech, May characterises all opponents as
perversely and irrationally opposed to any change.

> We must remember that there has always been initial distrust
> of new ideas and new technologies. Those who first displaced
> our planet from the centre of the universe were not greeted
> warmly. Indeed, hostility was expressed in more draconian
> terms than today: Bruno's burning; Galileo's enforced recan-
> tation and house arrest, with grudging apology a few centuries

later. The early history of vaccination shows not one, but two, distinct waves of distrust. The first, roughly two centuries ago, worried that vaccination might actually spread infection (as well as be beneficial to some), and caused fierce controversy. Vaccination with cowpox was also resisted, leading to public disturbances and newspaper cartoons fully in the 'Frankenstein Foods' idiom (of course, Mary Shelley had not yet written Frankenstein, but the little cows popping out of arms, as mad doctors attacked, captured the essentials). The second wave of widespread agitation occurred a little over 100 years ago, and had more of the character of a resistance by purveyors of nostrums, along with some physicians and others, to the early rise of a public health establishment deriving from advances in understanding the 'germ theory of disease'. The consequent public health programmes, and particularly childhood vaccinations, were thus resisted strongly by stakeholders in 'traditional knowledge' and instinctive beliefs.

Even the advent of the automobile, that mixed blessing which has liberated life in developed countries in so many ways, was greeted, particularly in the USA, with initial hostility.

Curiously, this draws on some of the same analogies (Galileo, vaccinations) as Tony Blair's speech. Like the invocation of Hitler, it is argument by loose association. There is no necessary association between either 'newness' or 'oldness' and desirability. To select cases of people irrationally rejecting change does not prove that all change is good. Just as different instances of fundamentalism would give a very different picture from those which May actually chooses, so would different instances of new technology. Opposition to nuclear weapons, for example, is a rather different case from opposition to vaccination programmes.

In terms of the communicative triangle, these passages are, like Blair's speech, much less about GM than about people's reaction to it, and they present the audience with a binary choice: either be for GM or join the forces of mindless ignorance and violent intolerance.

Recurrent patterns

So far we have analysed in some detail statements about biotechnology by four individuals (George W. Bush, Tony Blair, Prince Charles,

Lord May), albeit ones who claim to speak on behalf of others, and whose speeches and articles are produced in intensive consultation with advisers. Analysing the words of single people (and their speech-writers) in this way can undoubtedly provide many insights. But it can also, as already indicated, have disadvantages. It may reflect only the views or the style of that one individual and not be typical of the debate as a whole. In addition, if we extract a part of what they say from its context, it may not even be typical of that individual.

A different kind of language analysis which avoids these pitfalls is to survey larger quantities of data, to see if there are recurrent themes and patterns. Modern computer storage capacity and search programmes have revolutionised what can be done in this respect, both in the analysis of *what* is said (the points of view expressed) and *how* it is said (the words which are used). Computerised language corpus analysis (described in Chapter 1) can reveal recurrent word patterns. Data banks of documents and transcripts which have been coded manually for themes can be interrogated automatically to show which of these themes are most common.[5]

In a project[6] utilising these techniques, Elisa Pieri, Peter Robbins and I collected a large amount of data reflecting views on the communication of GM plant science. In the course of this project, we collected written material communicating and explaining GM research to non-experts, and we conducted lengthy interviews both with academic GM scientists with a variety of expertise and at various levels of seniority, and with 'non-experts' working in a university environment, including students, lecturers, technicians, canteen staff, administrators and senior managers. In addition, to provide further background information, we interviewed a number of 'outside advisers': senior scientists from the biotech industry (both Syngenta and Monsanto) and from anti-GM NGOs (GeneWatch UK, Friends of the Earth and Greenpeace). In total, forty-three people were interviewed (eighteen 'experts', fifteen 'non-experts' and ten 'outside advisers'), providing us with some fifty hours of recordings. Transcribed and stored electronically, these provided a corpus of approximately 300,000 words.

The most interesting part of our corpus, and the one which we studied most intensively, comprised the transcriptions of interviews with academic GM scientists. Our corpus enabled us to compare the way they spoke about GM both with non-experts and with more prominent GM proponents such as Tony Blair and Lord May – whose arguments and language we have already analysed fairly intensively. In each interview we first asked a number of general questions about attitudes to the technology, how GM issues are best communicated to non-expert audiences, the links between industry and universities, and other larger topics including the future of plant biotechnology and reasons for public reactions to GM. We then focused more specifically on language, asking interviewees to read a short text which sought to explain the technology, to argue for its benefits, and to discount fears of adverse consequences.

Just as there are disadvantages in concentrating on short extracts by one individual, so analysis of much larger language databases can also have a downside. It can merge individuals together, revealing general, recurrent or majority tendencies among interviewees rather than individual variation. What follows then is generalisation about the views of the scientists we interviewed. But some individuals and particular responses were at odds with these general tendencies, questioning or criticising, for example, the rigid categorisation which characterises the GM debate. How far the views we elicited are typical of GM scientists in general is difficult to say.

One interesting finding from our data is the unquestioning faith of the scientists we interviewed (echoing the views we have already analysed of Tony Blair and Lord May) that there are three clearly distinct categories of people in the GM debate: scientists, the public and opponents (including the press). These three groups are then stereotyped in quite striking ways. We shall deal with each in turn.

Scientists on scientists

Among the university scientists we interviewed, 'being a scientist' was generally seen as an either/or category, and no acknowledgement was made of any scientific competence outside a narrowly defined 'scientific community'. This was reflected as much in the use of words as in the views expressed. Thus the pronoun 'we', for example, almost always meant 'we scientists' (whether 'scientists' in general or 'GM scientists'). The word 'scientists' itself, moreover, almost always occurred alone, rather than in phrases such as 'scientists and other thinking people', 'scientists and other academics', etc. (By contrast, in the non-expert interviews, it was often linked with other groups, for example 'scientists and politicians'.) The general assumption was that the basics of the scientific method (simply conceived as induction from observation and experiment) are completely unfamiliar to outsiders and therefore always in need of explanation. No account was taken, in other words, of people in the process of becoming scientists, or people with some scientific training, of the use of scientific methods in the social sciences, and – perhaps most importantly – of the fact that not all scientists agree. Those scientists who are opposed to GM were simply reclassified on the grounds that they are not proper scientists!

Scientists on the public

The 'public' too were conceived as a homogeneous body: passive, emotional and ignorant. No allowance was made for any relevant expertise (in business, retail, politics, cookery, gardening, bird watching, etc.), or for any intermediate degrees of scientific knowledge or understanding. Nor was there any acknowledgement of any general critical ability in assessing the arguments of experts and pressure groups. Thus concordance analysis shows that the word 'public' typically occupies a semantically passive role (unlike words referring to either scientists or opponents of GM). The 'public', that is to say, are *done to* rather than *doers*, on the receiving end of other people's actions and words, rather than initiators themselves. On the occasions when the word 'public' is the subject of a clause, it typically – as in Tony Blair's speech – governs verbs of emotion such as 'is concerned about', 'feels', 'believes'. One particularly telling instance, from which we took the title of an article on this topic,[7] occurred in the following comment: 'but all of those things have changed in the way scientists think and the public feels. Now perhaps scientists haven't been very good at telling the public how they've changed . . .'.

Here we see not only the typical contrast between scientists' rationality ('think') and the public's emotion ('feels') but also one of activity and passivity (discussion involves scientists 'telling the public'). The public, then, were typically categorised as emotional rather than rational, and passively vulnerable to manipulation by self-interested opponents: including politicians, the press and NGOs.

Public opposition to GM was attributed to ignorance and consequently as something to be remedied by education. On more than one occasion, this characterisation was backed up by anecdotes of farcical encounters with particularly uninformed members of the public: a common one concerned people who are worried that they may be 'eating DNA'. Here is a typical example:

> I had a lady from a magazine ring me up about genetic manipulation and said their readers were worried, and they were worried about this fact that they were eating DNA. And

I said, 'well, look, you know, OK, but we're eating DNA all the time you know.' 'Are we? Really? We're eating DNA?' And I mean I can understand. I'm not criticising her at all or belittling her, but she had no idea that everything was full of DNA.

It was also claimed that the 'public' has no understanding of risk, naively believing in, and foolishly demanding, unscientific reassurances of 'zero risk'; to be told, in other words, that GM is 'absolutely safe'.[8] Here is what three different scientists had to say:

1. The no risk culture – this idea that the public feels or that what they ought to be assured of is that there is no risk – is a kind of ostrich's head in the sand situation because life isn't risk free. But people want to be told that something is absolutely safe. And of course you can't tell people that something is absolutely safe. All you can say is that up to now it's been reasonably safe and that very few mistakes have happened or errors have happened or accidents have happened.

2. People irrationally they say, 'Is there any risk associated with this?' And you can't put your hand on your heart as a scientist and say there is no risk. You have to say, 'Well our experiments have not shown anything that we need to be worried about.' And of course the public are quite rightly concerned about those kind of statements, whereas if they're more familiar with what's happening and things, they would perhaps understand those statements more.

3. As far as people are concerned risks are reality. People do not generally have a conception of risk. They can't understand risk. If there's a risk of something happening, then they will assume it's going to happen to them.

In this emphasis on public ignorance, the scientists we interviewed subscribe to what has been called a 'Deficit Model' of public understanding,[9] in which opposition to a new technology is attributed wholly to a lack of knowledge. Here are two representative quotations from two of our interviewees.

1. There are relatively few people that are absolutely against no matter what. Those that are tend to be less well informed in general than those that've taken a more measured view.

2. I would say that it's far more seeking to provide information so that people become more able to be rational in the areas that they are worried about and become more relaxed in the areas that are really frankly nothing to worry about.

This is a very widespread attitude among scientists, appearing frequently in talks and lectures supporting GM. This, for example, appeared in a pamphlet advertising a talk on 'Communicating science' by Professor Colin Blakemore, who was at that time Chairman of the British Association for the Advancement of Science:[10]

For 15 years, Britain's scientific establishment has encouraged scientists to communicate with the public, originally to improve the public understanding of science, and now to promote dialogue on controversial issues. Public understanding is better here than in many parts of Europe, but, paradoxically, confidence in science is inversely related to understanding, and anti-scientific attitudes are rampant.

And here is Professor Janet Bainbridge, Chair, UK Government Advisory Committee on Novel Foods and Processes:[11] 'Most people do not even know what a gene is. Sometimes my young son wants to cross the road when it's dangerous – sometimes you have to tell people what's best for them.'

This same notion of one-way communication characterises government pronouncements too. According to British Environment Secretary Margaret Beckett, the function of the government-funded 'GM nation?' debate in Britain would be to 'ascertain . . . [and] address . . . gaps and uncertainties in public knowledge' and 'deepen public understanding of all the issues surrounding GM'[12] – rather than to listen to, or take advice from, members of the public.

What is strange about this deficit model encountered so frequently among scientists is how unscientific it is, as it is voiced without reference to any evidence. Indeed, although some quantitative research has correlated ignorance of technologies with negative attitudes,[13] there is other quantitative research[14] and a good deal of qualitative research adopting more open questions, and less quantitative techniques which have found exactly the opposite: that knowledge of technicalities does not lead to increased acceptance.[15] Most strikingly of all, the report[16] on the government-funded debate on GM in Britain, discussing the results of a 'narrow but deep' study of people who were neither particularly well informed nor committed[17] on the issue of GM found that the more information they acquired, the more hardened their views became.

Among our expert interviewees, the claim that the public lack knowledge and can only engage on an emotional level with the issues was then key to a further argumentative twist, allowing public opposition to be explained as entirely created by the media and NGOs, rather than as ever being a spontaneous, considered or autonomous response.

> A lot of this has been driven by green pressure groups. And I think they have been playing on fears of the unknown. And I think that a lot of the rather sensationalist press has got a lot to do with the very anti feelings about GM in this country at the moment. Because scare stories sell papers, good news doesn't.

To a degree, this characterisation of public opinion appeared to free the GM scientists we interviewed from having to engage with public disquiet. When asked directly, many of them spoke favourably of the increased emphasis on communicating with non-experts, although what seemed to be envisaged was one-way communication in which members of the public would be educated.

> I think the same's true with GM. There's no point just discussing GM because that's in a vacuum. To discuss GM you have to have people knowing what's happening in genetics, what's happening in biology, what's happening with the food position, what does nutrition mean, etcetera.

Scientists on the opposition

The third category, 'opponents', was also kept, implicitly and explicitly, separate from the other two. It is as though there are no members of the public or scientists who are also campaigning opponents. Opposition to GM was seen as emanating from self-interested individuals and organisations acting upon a malleable and passive public, rather than from the public itself. The two main sources of opposition were seen as campaigning NGOs and the press, and to a lesser extent supermarkets and politicians, all of whom were judged to be acting in their own interests and making decisions without authority on the public's behalf. Very noticeably, there was a marked focus upon certain sources, with little attempt to understand the range and types of opposition, or to respond to serious and scientifically informed arguments against GM. Over half of the references to the press, for example, focus upon the single phrase 'Frankenstein foods' used in the *Daily Mail*, while there are virtually no references to more thoughtful expressions of doubt or opposition. References to anti-GM NGOs are almost entirely to Greenpeace, while Friends of the Earth and GeneWatch UK are mentioned much less frequently and only in conjunction with Greenpeace. NGOs are characterised as launching campaigns in order to maintain membership and finance their organisation and salaries.[18] Journalists are seen as fickle, unconcerned with truth, and motivated only by the need for a 'good story'. Anti-GM protestors and activists are less frequently mentioned, though when they are, it is in condemnatory terms. On one occasion they are equated with terrorists and fascists in terms reminiscent of Lord May.

> You got terrorists come along and trashing it. Our crops last year were trashed twice you know. What grounds do we have for rational scientific debate if NGOs and their associates conduct and condone this type of activity? I mean quite frankly it's outrageous. And you know in the 1940s they burnt books and now they tear up plants.

A striking aspect of our interviews with GM scientists, in contrast to those with non-specialists, was the general dearth of reference to major arguments in the wider national and international debate. Decisions about the introduction of GM technology were perceived as almost entirely safety oriented. As far as other types of argument were concerned, there was some vague awareness of ethical objections to GM technology, but these were generally considered to be religious and/or caricatured as beyond the reach of reasoned argument. Most striking of all was the virtual absence of reference to the political and economic implications of GM, how policy decisions are made about it, the nature and speed of its implementation, or accusations of improper influence being exerted by governments, corporations or scientific bodies – even though these arguments all feature prominently in the anti-GM literature and in reactions of the public to GM.

As observed at the opening of this chapter, there is a tendency for scientists to see their way of viewing things as different from others', and to seek to keep it separate. Yet ironically they do not seem to succeed. There is a marked tendency for the views of pro-GM scientists and pro-GM politicians to echo and replicate each other. This is especially true, as we have seen, in their views of the public and the opposition. There are only three possible positions, with no overlaps and no alternatives.

Most striking of all is the considerable contradiction between the noble aspiration of science to base opinions upon the impartial and rational assessment of evidence and pro-GM scientists' own descriptions and assessments of the opponents of GM and their arguments. Particularly ironic is the unscientific nature of the arguments – emotive language, false analogies, loose associations and the selective use of examples – all apparently in defence of science.

3

JOURNALISTS

It is possible to divide those involved in the GM debate into very broad categories: politicians, scientists, journalists, corporations, protestors, NGOs, the public. Yet, although this is useful, it brings its own dangers. For both sides in the debate – at its most simplistic – it is enough just to label people in this way for their views to appear compromised or invalid. Thus for the anti-GM lobby, 'biotech companies' and sometimes even 'scientists' become terms of derision; on the pro-GM side the negative terms are 'protestors' and 'campaigners'. For the university scientists whose views were reported at the end of the last chapter, to be a member of 'the public' is to be ignorant and irrational, while the labels 'politicians' and 'journalists' were for them synonymous with duplicity and smooth-talking opportunism – in contrast to their own stolid inarticulate honesty. Each group creates its own mythology of what is happening, a narrative in which the overriding metaphor is one of opposing armies (as in Tony Blair's 'overrun by protestors') rather than of a real debate in which people try to understand each other's opinions. So although I am using these categories in this book as an organising device, I hope also to show, by delving into the identity and language of each of them in turn, that rigid categories, and perceptions of people as insiders and outsiders, can also prevent us from hearing what is really being said. All too often in the GM debate, it is with the act of labelling someone else or oneself (as protestor, scientist, journalist, etc.) that communication suffers most, and it becomes harder to see clearly what is being talked about rather than how the speaker wants it to be seen. The subject of this chapter – 'the press' – and the people who construct it – 'journalists' – is another case in point.

It is common to talk about 'The Press' – often written like that, with initial capitals – as though it was a single institution producing one homogenous discourse. In our interviews with scientists for example (described in the last chapter), we found many of them talking about 'the press' as though newspapers were all the same. But a moment's reflection shows that this is misleading. Newspapers are not only very different from each other, there are many different types of discourse within them with a variety of functions and forms. And this is not just a question of the classic divisions: reports, features, editorials, letters and so on. Even within these broad traditional categories we find very different realisations.

In a second research project[1] on the discourse of GM, Elisa Pieri, Peter Robbins and I monitored the British press for its discussion of GM food and crops. The most intensive phase of this exercise was during the period January to July 2003. We collected every article which even mentioned GM from four British newspapers: *The Times*, the *Guardian*, the *Daily Mail* and the *Sun*. We chose these particular newspapers to represent the traditional division of British newspapers into broadsheet and tabloid, and for their differences of view on GM. *The Times* and the *Sun* were in the main pro-GM and the *Guardian* and the *Daily Mail* in the main anti-GM. All in all, we collected 446 articles and letters,[2] stored on computer in a way which enabled quick automated searches for frequent word uses and patterns of the kind described in Chapter 1. Though the resulting corpus was a large one (over 259,000 words), it was still possible, though time-consuming, to study it through close reading. Both these operations – automated computer searching and continuous reading – have a curious and illuminating effect. Articles on a single topic are no longer separated in time and space. They no longer come at us in a haphazard way, mixed in with other events and topics, part of a hotchpotch of short pieces, to be carelessly skimmed and discarded. Instead they form a continuous document in which one can easily move backwards and forwards to cross-reference and compare, creating a very different impression from that of day-by-day reading. The nature of news is transformed. Patterns and themes begin to emerge which would be lost in the conventional processing of the press. It becomes much easier to assess the 'mood' of each newspaper, and its particular 'line' on a given topic. (Readers who access thematically dedicated websites such as those of the 'Guardian Unlimited' Special Reports or the BBC news pages will already be familiar with this phenomenon.)

	LEFT			RIGHT	
BROADSHEET	The Guardian	The Independent	The Times	The Daily Telegraph	EDUCATED MIDDLE CLASS
				The Daily Mail	
				The Express	
					LESS EDUCATED
TABLOID	The Mirror			The Sun	WORKING CLASS

Figure 1 Traditional newspaper alignments.

Traditionally, the British press has been divided into tabloid and broadsheet, radical and conservative, and these divisions have in turn been associated with the social class, level of education and political opinions of the readership,[3] so that, broadly speaking, newspapers might be placed within or across the quadrants of a schematic representation, as shown in Figures 1 and 2.

But this simple categorisation soon begins to fall apart, at least in the contemporary world. (Whether it ever worked in the past is a moot point.) Among our four British newspapers, the most interesting in this respect is the *Daily Mail*. Situated in format and style, and in depth of coverage, half-way between a tabloid and broadsheet, it has long been synonymous with the most conservative, middle-brow mind-set: reactionary, anti-intellectual, anti-European, xenophobic, assertive of the 'common-sense' values of middle England. The phrase '*Daily Mail* reader' has become a byword for such attitudes. Yet the *Daily Mail* became in the 1990s the most vociferous media opponent of GM crops and food, the coiner of the infamous phrase 'Frankenstein food' (28 January 1999), and the platform (as we have already seen in Chapter 1) for the anti-GM views of Prince Charles (himself an anomalous combination of reactionary and progressive). In some ways this stance can be regarded as merely a continuation of the newspaper's conservatism, seeing GM as a superfluous and alien intrusion into a traditional way of life. Yet it also brought it some strange new

	ANTI-GM		PRO-GM	
BROADSHEET	The Guardian		The Times	EDUCATED MIDDLE CLASS
	The Daily Mail			
				LESS EDUCATED
TABLOID			The Sun	WORKING CLASS

Figure 2 GM newspaper alignments in our survey.

bedfellows. For among the other opponents of GM are many of the newspaper's old enemies: the European Union, religious fundamentalists, 'Old Labour', intellectuals, environmentalists, proponents of alternative lifestyles, and direct action groups committed to civil disobedience. To a degree, then, the GM debate, like numerous other issues, has undermined traditional divisions by bringing together conservative and radical opinion under the same banner. Though it is possible to see this as a specifically British phenomenon, reflecting opposition from both the 'first way' (Tory capitalism and traditionalism) and the 'second way' (Old Labour socialism) to the ascendant high-tech, pro-business, US-style globalisation advocated by New Labour,[4] it is equally possible to regard it as indicative of a more general global realignment and blurring of distinctions between left and right, traditionalist and radical, in the acceleration of which the GM issue is one of a number of catalysts.

The stance of the other three newspapers in our sample is perhaps more predictable and less surprising, though it too can reflect some change of allegiance. The *Guardian*, though it published both pro- and anti-GM opinion, was persistent in its critical left-of-centre stand and its scepticism of the motives of both government and business.[5] The broadsheet *The Times* and the tabloid *Sun* were, predictably, generally pro-GM, reflecting perhaps the views of their owner Rupert Murdoch.[6] Yet like the *Daily Mail*, the *Sun* and *The Times* were also drawn into uncharacteristic alliances. The *Sun* found itself singing the praises of left-wing anti-GM MP Michael Meacher for his criticisms of the EU[7] and the traditionalist *Times* found itself carrying outspoken criticism of the heir to the throne.[8]

Let us begin with a consideration of some of the apparently more marginal, even light-hearted references to the topic of GM, and of how one particular story, which appeared in all four newspapers, was presented. Here is the *Sun*, characteristically jovial and snappy:

BRITAIN'S FAVOURITE FRUIT IS DYING OUT
YES, WE'LL HAVE NO BANANAS
BANANAS could become extinct because a vicious disease is wiping the fruit out.
The fungus, Sigatoka, is devastating plants in Africa.
And experts say it threatens to spread to all edible varieties of banana, killing them within ten years.
Fans of our great Banana Diet will be relieved supplies will be around long enough to help them shed weight. . . .

Emile Frison is top banana at the International Network for the Improvement of Banana and Plantain.

He told *New Scientist* magazine that the only hope of saving edible bananas may be to create controversial GM versions – a new Frankenstein food. That would involve taking a gene from a disease-resistant, non-edible banana and injecting it into the threatened fruit.

(*Sun*, 16 January 2003)

The *Mail*, having presumably used the same source and having a similar sense of humour, not only gives the same facts but also makes the same allusion to the old music-hall song: 'YES, WE'LL HAVE NO BANANAS . . .' (*Daily Mail*, 16 January 2003). Significantly, however, it leaves reference to a possible GM solution until the very end, presenting it only as the opinion of *some* experts, implying perhaps that others may disagree, and including a reference to consumer reluctance to buy GM food.

Some experts believe the only hope for the long-term future of the banana may be genetic modification. But until now the big banana companies have refused to countenance GM research for fear of putting customers off.

The *Guardian* too begins its report in light-hearted vein and with the same allusion – though much more ponderously expressed:

It is a freakish, doped-up, mutant clone which hasn't had sex for thousands of years – and the strain may be about to tell on the nation's fruitbowl favourite. Scientists based in France have warned that, without radical and swift action, in 10 years' time we really could have no bananas.

(*Guardian*, 16 January 2003)

But it goes further and is more specific than the *Daily Mail* in doubting GM as the only solution: 'One possibility is GM bananas, but growers fear consumer resistance. The big growers are pinning their hopes on better fungicides.'

Only *The Times* avoids the obvious joke. It carries the same story, written up by its science correspondent Mark Henderson, in a less flippant manner than its rivals, though showing the same confidence in the GM solution as the *Sun*.

BANANAS 'WILL SLIP INTO EXTINCTION WITHOUT GM'

THE banana could be slipping towards extinction within ten years, unless genetic modification can protect it from the scourge of fungal diseases, according to scientists.

(*The Times*, 16 January 2003)

But what are the first three reports doing with their humorous openings and their flippant references – 'Yes, we'll have no bananas . . .', 'Fans of our great Banana Diet', 'Emile Frison is top banana', 'hasn't had sex for thousands of years', 'the nation's fruit-bowl favourite' and so on? Is their primary purpose to inform or amuse? The banana fungus is undoubtedly a very serious problem, not only for banana growers and retailers worldwide, but because it affects a major food source and is symptomatic of how, in a global agricultural system, local crises can become global disasters. Yet it is presented here very much tongue in cheek, and as though it were a problem only for Britain ('Britain's favourite fruit', 'our great banana diet'). And in addition to its entertainment value, it seems also intended to persuade by describing a clear case of a GM technology being put to good use. The point was certainly persuasive for at least one *Sun* reader who dutifully responded with the following letter

> Dear *Sun*
> AFTER all the bad news we've had so far this year it was so disappointing to read that my favourite fruit, the humble banana, is in grave danger of dying out.
> I'm not usually in favour of GM versions of foodstuffs but on this occasion I would make an exception.
> HARRIET SHORT. Wolverhampton
> (*Sun*, 25 January 2003)

The banana story typifies a certain kind of article about GM, which can actually be found in all four newspapers (though less frequently in the *Guardian*). Compared with the major topics of the debate such as the environmental impacts of GM crops and the health effects of GM food, they deal with relatively peripheral, albeit sometimes very important, consequences of GM technology. Here is a selection.

Decaffeinated brews could soon be cheaper and tastier after Japanese scientists grew GM coffee plants with 70 per cent less caffeine than normal.

(*Sun*, 19 June 2003)

THE world's first genetically modified cigarettes went on sale yesterday amid claims that they will help millions of smokers to quit the habit.

(*Daily Mail*, 28 January 2003)

ALLERGY-FREE PEANUTS
GM variety could end danger to children
THE threat of peanut allergies could soon be wiped out by genetic engineering, scientists have revealed.

(*Daily Mail*, 17 February 2003)

PLANTS MAY WARN OF BIO-TERROR
American scientists are developing a genetically modified plant that would change colour when exposed to biological or chemical weapons.

Researchers at Colorado State University have won a grant of nearly £300,000 from the US Department of Defence to investigate if it is possible to produce 'plant sentries' for malls and offices to provide early warning of a bio-terrorist attack.

(*The Times*, 15 February 2003)

HERE KITTY KITTY: JONATHAN HEDDLE ON A NEW CURE FOR THOSE WHO ARE ALLERGIC TO FURRY PETS
One American company recently revealed that it was trying to produce a genetically modified cat that did not produce the allergenic protein. This drew strong protests from animal rights groups and it is uncertain if the cat will ever be produced.

(*Guardian*, 11 March 2003)

GM THERAPY OFFERS HOPE OF SEX AFTER PROSTATE CANCER
GENE therapy could help men undergoing surgery for prostate cancer to enjoy normal sex lives, scientists said yesterday.

Four out of five patients who have their prostate removed suffer erectile dysfunction because crucial nerves are severed. But laboratory experiments using a genetically modified version of the virus causing cold sore infections have been encouraging.

(*Daily Mail*, 29 April 2003)

GM GRASS PLAN
Hay fever sufferers may soon be able to breathe more easily after the development of genetically modified grass that will not trigger allergic reactions. Scientists in Australia have engineered two strains of rye grass without two of the crucial allergens that cause hay fever.

(*The Times*, 19 June 2003)

Despite their light-hearted or incidental tone, all of these reports strongly imply reasons to support GM. Each one concerns something self-evidently beneficial: preservation of the banana, reduction of drug use, relief for allergy sufferers, help for cancer patients, detection of biological attack. Another such story (which ran significantly in *The Times*) is presumably intended to imply the hypocrisy of EU opposition to GM:

EURO NOTES ARE GENETICALLY MODIFIED, SCIENTISTS REVEAL
Sceptics who derided the euro as an artificial currency have been right all along: its banknotes are printed on genetically modified cotton.

Though the European Union has some of the toughest GM regulations in the world, it has ignored the transgenic fibres in its own currency. The engineered banknotes are not even labelled. Most modern banknotes are printed on cotton-based paper, as it is both highly durable and difficult to forge. Sterling uses a mixture of cotton and linen rag, while the euro is 100 per cent cotton.

(*The Times*, 1 January 2003)

One thing which is striking about these short items is how often the developments they report are only speculative. They refer to possible findings, not actual ones, as the following phrases reveal: 'could soon be cheaper', 'amid claims that they will help', 'could end danger', 'could soon be wiped out', 'are developing', 'that would change', 'to investigate if it is possible', 'could help men', 'have been encouraging', 'may soon be able to breathe more easily', 'trying to produce a genetically modified cat'.

None of these reports, in other words (apart from the one about the euro), referred at the time to actual facts, only to possible ones. Corpus analysis of the entire archive reveals that this is a common feature of GM stories, though one which may be missed in casual readings which mistakenly conflate speculation with fact.[9]

Despite its very serious take on the banana crisis, *The Times* is no stranger to flippant humour. For example, in its letters section, itself a national institution, it is fond of including brief, supposedly light-hearted comments on topical issues. Though often phrased in hyper-correct standard English, these are as trivial and dismissive as anything in the tabloids. (Whether they are as funny is a matter of personal taste.)

> Sir, Having just spent an hour on my allotment, I am convinced that The Really Useful Genetic Engineering Company would be less controversially, and more profitably, employed designing a slug that would eat weeds.
> I remain, Sir, yours faithfully . . .
>
> (1 July 2003)

> Sir, I don't know much about GM crops (letters, July 3, etc.), but I am sure that a fortune awaits whoever can modify grass to grow just two inches and then stop.
>
> (9 July 2003)

These particular letters also give the GM issue a particular twist. Writing from the viewpoint of the amateur British gardener, they present nature (in the shape of slugs, weeds and grass) as something which humanity struggles to control.

There were times during 2003 when coverage of the GM debate was eclipsed by other international events, notably the war in Iraq. If we look at a simple list of GM-focused articles from the newspapers we studied during this period, we see, not surprisingly, a marked decrease during March and April, the months in which the news, in Britain as elsewhere in the world, contained little other than the war and its aftermath. But the topic of GM by no means disappeared, certainly not to the extent that proponents may have hoped. There were plenty of GM events, both before, during and after the war, which continued to keep it newsworthy. In Britain there was the build-up to the official 'GM nation?' public debate organised by the government, the sudden suggestion by the Environment Secretary Margaret Beckett, significantly at the height of the Iraq crisis, that she might proceed with eighteen applications to import and grow GM crops,[10] the sacking of the Environment Minister Michael Meacher, his subsequent denunciation of GM,[11] the publication of the scientific review report[12] and the government's own policy unit reports,[13] and the results of the Farm Scale Evaluations.[14] Internationally, there was continuing discussion of the decision by the Zambian and other African governments to turn down US food aid in late 2002 because it was GM grain. At the World Trade Organisation, in the lead-up to its September summit of 2003, there was ongoing tension between the largely anti-GM EU and the resolutely pro-GM Bush administration in the USA. Meanwhile the British government defied both the EU majority and public opinion at home to express support for the US line. It was a scenario which uncannily mirrored UN divisions in the build-up to the war in Iraq.

A cynical view of 'the Press' might consign these GM issues to a list of replacement topics for journalists to fill in gaps when readers tired of the other recurrent news items: terrorism, Iraq, Palestine, the EU, educational standards, immigration, public services. And in the interviews we conducted with anti-GM campaigners they often expressed exactly that view, that the GM issue was often forced out of the news by other more immediate dangers. But the relationship of the GM debate to other news is more complicated. As we read through the newspaper articles of this period we see how the apparently disparate topics of the moment were increasingly woven together into a single narrative in which GM was a significant symbolic component. In this way GM never left the news, even when it was not the immediate topic. It was mixed in with, or used to illustrate, other domains, just as they – especially Western fears of terrorism and Islamic fundamentalism – are invoked to describe the GM debate itself.

This 'mixing' (in both senses of the word) is characteristic of both sides, and it is done both metaphorically and literally. Thus on the anti-GM side, we find Prince Charles, in metaphorical vein, talking of 'genetically modified' urban planning,[15] while Tom Dyckhoff uses the same term disparagingly to talk about bureaucratic language, citing the word 'de-densify' as an example of the 'gaping fields of genetically modified developers' vernacular' (*The Times*, 1 July 2003). In more literal terms, Catherine Bennett highlights the significant overlap between the anti-war and the anti-GM movements. In an article deriding the anti-war slogan 'Not in My Name' as too weak, she describes it as 'more suited to use by picky consumers who define themselves, say, by their disapproval of GM foods, or boycotting of Starbucks . . . than by a mass movement aiming to change the views of a legitimate government' (*Guardian*, 23 January 2003).

Tony Juniper, the incoming director of Friends of the Earth,[16] and Michael Meacher in an interview with the *Ecologist*,[17] both explicitly link environmental issues with the impending military campaign. Meacher, after losing his ministerial post later in the year,[18] went on to write, with the benefit of inside knowledge, two devastating attacks on the Blair government policy, accusing it of distorting evidence. Significantly one was on GM food,[19] the other on the decision to go to war.[20]

So the association of issues in the news can be either very loose and metaphorical or very explicit and literal. In the brief, somewhat peripheral articles cited above, we can see a number of examples. The 'exposé' of EU hypocrisy for printing banknotes on GM cotton links the EU with the anti-GM lobby; the item 'Plants may warn of bioterror' enlists GM science as an ally in 'the war on terrorism'. The coinage 'bioterrorism' is used in a rather different and much more sinister way by each side to refer to the other. Thus a letter to *The Times* (6 June 2003) observes that 'The main hazard that GM crops present is that they attract crop-destroying attention-seeking bio-terrorists.'

Meanwhile, on the other side, Rama Lakshmi, writing of reaction to GM in India, observes that 'However, opponents claimed that the environmental impact of genetically modified crops amounted to "bioterrorism." Ecologists said altered genes may enter the food chain, as many Indian villagers use cottonseed oil in their cooking' (*Guardian Weekly*, 8 May 2003).

The best way, it seems, in the era of 'the war on terrorism', is to try to identify your opponents as part of the enemy. It is a tactic we have seen already. Tony Blair, Lord May and a number of the scientists we interviewed all linked opposition to GM with enemy attacks.

The better to understand how such links work in extended argument, let us examine a representative article in more detail. It is an attack on the man whose name is, significantly, the most frequent proper noun, and thus the most talked about person, in our newspaper corpus.[21]

ISN'T THERE A CHEMICAL SPRAY FOR MEACHER BLIGHT?
Crackpots declaring that 'the end of the world is nigh' are nothing new. But that notion is no longer the preserve of religious

zealots or sci-fi fantasists. It now seems to be the position of a government minister – Michael Meacher. And the weapons of mass destruction that Mr Meacher is most worried about are you and I. While attention has focused elsewhere, the Environment Minister appears to have launched an evangelical mission, preaching that we are in danger of destroying our world through the advance of science and new technologies. In a speech last week he speculated that man-made global warming could 'make our planet uninhabitable'. 'We are the virus' infecting the Earth's body, he said, concluding that 'this is the first time that a species has been at risk of generating its own demise'. In an interview to be published today in the *Ecologist* magazine, Meacher says that genetically modified (GM) crop technology could pose 'totally unpredicted problems'.

There is talk of Meacher resigning because of his isolation within the Government.

His recent statements certainly read like a suicide note for our species, never mind for his career. Yet far from being, as he has previously suggested, 'a lone voice in the wilderness', the 'very, very cautious' Mr Meacher speaks for a powerful current of very, very cautious opinion today. Its views are a man-made virus that, allowed to go unchecked, could prove more destructive of civilised society than any foreign terrorist.

Take the question of GM technologies, now back in the news as the Government tries to sponsor a wider debate. Although Britain's controversial field-scale trials are supposed to be investigating the impact of GM crops on insects, slugs, snails, weeds and the like, this issue has never really been about those things. It is about humanity, and how far we aspire to rise above that which crawls upon the earth.

Meacher puts the case for an, err, sluggish approach to human progress in his *Ecologist* interview. Arguing that, for the past quarter million years, 'we have been feeding ourselves perfectly adequately since overcoming problems of hunger in our early existence', he concludes 'GM is not necessary'. Which, indeed, it is not. By the same token, of course, steam engines, electric lights, aircraft, television and the internet were 'not necessary' for us to carry on 'feeding ourselves perfectly adequately' in our cosy caves and hovels.

Not satisfied with lowering our expectations of scientific and social progress, the fashionable doctrine espoused by Meacher the preacher also threatens to degrade democracy. In his interview, he implies that his colleague, Lord Sainsbury of Turville, Under Secretary for Science and Innovation, cannot be trusted to be objective about GM since he has links with the biotech industries (that is, he knows something about the stuff). Yet Meacher and his allies have been keen to subject policy on GM to the influence of other unelected, unaccountable interests – the environmental and consumer lobby groups.

The director of one anti-GM group, GeneWatch, recently expressed the hope that new Labour's openness to consulting such organisations might 'change the way we do democracy'. Indeed it might 'do democracy' altogether, by giving the casting vote to parasitical eco-groups.

What motivates the Meacherites (like just about every protest movement today) is the obsession with avoiding risk. It remains to be seen whether the Government will stand up to them. Let us hope this is a battle Tony Blair is prepared to fight with the determination he seems to reserve for foreign fields.

If the doom-mongers get their way, the end of the world will not be nigh, but it might just feel as though it is.

(Mick Hume, *The Times*, 17 February 2003)

Such a polemical article is likely to elicit strong approval or disapproval. In practice, any assessment is likely to depend on the reader's own views on Michael Meacher, environmental policy and GM. It need not necessarily be the case, however, that an argument is judged only by its conclusions. Whatever one's views on GM or any other controversial issue, one might still praise the way a case is made despite disagreeing with its outcome, or one might acknowledge the force of *some* of what is being said without accepting the whole.

In this article, however, assessment is further complicated. For judgement is likely to be based, more than in most cases, not primarily on what is being said, and its accuracy and rationality, but also on how that content is phrased and presented, and why. The flamboyant style and hyperbolic claims could suggest that its purpose is more to entertain, or to rally existing support, than to inform or persuade. Its audience is those who, in a general sense, already agree. Indeed, it is hard to imagine that any pro–Meacher readers would change their view after reading this article, or that trying to make them do so was among the aims of the author. A problem at the outset of this analysis is thus one of genre. If its primary function is to entertain, or to indulge the views of those who already agree, then it seems misguided to assess it by standards of rationality and presentation of evidence to which it does not aspire. In the same way, one would not castigate a children's story for being fantastical or a nonsense rhyme for being illogical. On the contrary, in these genres it is exactly such qualities which might lead to positive appraisal. On the other hand, it could be argued that, in matters of such urgency and consequence as the impact of a new technology, and in newspaper feature articles in general, discussion should be both factual and reasonable. Part of the problem in analysing this article is that it is not really clear what its terms are or by what standards it should be judged. This itself works to the author's advantage and is indicative of his skill, as any criticism is open to the charge of taking matters too seriously or too literally.

Very striking in the development of its argument is the number of comparisons the article contains, and the ways in which they appear, disappear and reappear as it progresses. The author turns round Meacher's own claim that humanity is a virus, making Meacher the blight, and the environmental pressure groups 'parasitical'. This metaphor is apt in its own way, and clever, as Meacher and the 'eco-groups' are indeed trying to destroy a certain kind of crop. Next Meacher is compared to a religious fanatic, a comparison which later reappears in the rhyming epithet 'Meacher the preacher'. Then it is claimed that Meacher was comparing 'you and I' to 'weapons of mass destruction'. In a sense this is merely a logical extension of Meacher's own claims. A virus which wipes out other species does indeed cause mass destruction, and 'humanity' and 'you and I' are synonymous in an article which could, in theory, be read by anybody. Yet, given that this article was written at the time of the build-up to the Iraq war, this reference to the pretext for that war, which seems so logical, is also disingenuous, as it introduces a parallel, which is amplified later, between the conflict over GM and the conflict over Iraq. Like the comparison of Meacher to a 'blight', it turns the tables, so that 'civilized society' is threatened not only from outside, but also by 'weapons of mass destruction' which are inside it. The suggestion is that there is an 'enemy within'. This connection is amplified at the beginning of the next paragraph, where it is claimed that Meacher has launched this attack 'while attention is focused elsewhere', taking advantage, in other words, of the government's preoccupation with Iraq. The debate is set firmly within the context of the military crisis.

The comparisons continue to multiply and magnify. Meacher's statements are like 'a suicide note for our species' and by implication for his own career. He speaks for a 'powerful current' of opinion which is a 'man-made virus' and is worse than 'any foreign terrorist'. Given the mood of the times, this verges on being a very serious charge – and the writer is careful to compare only Meacher's views, rather the man himself, to a 'foreign terrorist'. Next, in an ingenious twist, Meacher and the anti-GM lobby are compared to the very creatures they fear that GM will harm, for, if GM and other technologies allow humanity to 'rise above that which crawls upon the earth', then those who oppose the rise are like those creatures themselves – a point reinforced by the structure of the next sentence, with its mocking insertion of 'err' before the epithet 'sluggish' to describe Meacher's 'approach to human progress'.

It is an extraordinarily dense array of insinuating metaphors and equivalences, in which every point which Meacher has made, or is interpreted as having made, is turned against him. Much of its power is achieved through wit and bombast rather than reasoned argument. Indeed, one of its great ironies – possibly deliberate – is that while accusing Meacher of preaching it resorts itself to some blatantly rhetorical and evangelical tricks, setting off, through its choice of wording, biblical and poetic echoes of its own:

> a lone voice in the wilderness . . . how far we aspire to rise above that which crawls upon the earth. . . . Let us hope this is a battle Tony Blair is prepared to fight with the determination he seems to reserve for foreign fields.

We might describe this opening argument as largely poetic and witty. With this reservation in mind, however, if we strip the remainder of the article of its embellishments – which is, granted, to take away its *raison d'être* – there are, in among all the showmanship, at least two more substantial points. First, the argument that GM technology is unnecessary is rebutted with reference to beneficial technologies which are also unnecessary. Second, Meacher is accused of double standards in implying that Lord Sainsbury should not make ministerial decisions about GM because of his links with unelected business interests, when he (Meacher) has links with unelected environmentalist groups. This last point also includes the barbed aside: 'that is, he [Lord Sainsbury] knows something about the stuff'. This implies, perhaps, that Meacher and the environmental groups do not know 'something about the stuff', and should defer in decision-making to those with technical knowledge. The superfluous use of Sainsbury's full title 'Lord Sainsbury of Turville, Under Secretary for Science and Innovation' seems further to emphasise the perceived disparity.

Though expressed with great verve, the points in this article are not particularly original, and we can find them repeated with regularity by the pro-GM lobby. Comparisons with other technological and scientific discoveries which were initially rejected is particularly frequent. We have met it already in the speeches of Tony Blair and Lord May. Reference to Galileo is a particular favourite. Here is the Chairman of Unilever on opposition to GM: 'It seems sometimes that Europe has taken a step backwards into a time when the scientific discoveries of Galileo could be regarded as incorrect on the basis of dogma alone.'[22]

Another is vaccination. Here is one of the scientists we interviewed in our first project:

> People are generally frightened or uncertain of change and there are many examples of where new technology has been attacked and has been controversial, for instance certainly in the field of agriculture and artificial insemination there were sermons preached in the churches against this new and unnatural technology. When Jenner first was working on his smallpox vaccine there were anti-vaccination societies and people didn't want milk pasteurised because it would do all sorts of horrible things to milk and it might be dangerous and so on. Now all of those technologies have now been proven sound, safe and of good value.

Similar references occur in letters to *The Times*. Philip Stott, Professor Emeritus of Biogeography in the University of London, writing about Prince Charles, remarks that:

> Sadly, he, and far too many others who should know better, have become the genetically regressive symbols of a society frightened of its own shadow – nostalgic for a past that never was in an increasingly risk-averse world.
>
> Alas, poor science, I knew thee well. DVDs, antibiotics, dentistry, vaccination – how you have threatened us with constant disaster. How marvellous our lives would be if you had never been invented.
>
> (*The Times*, 6 May 2003)

Here is a letter published later in the year from Professor Derek Burke:

Sir, Dr Chris Smaje (letter, June 20) asks why we should 'take the risk' over GM technology, because nobody can be absolutely certain that there will be no risk to someone at some time in the future. The same question could have been asked about railways, the internal combustion engine, vaccination, the use of antibiotics or mobile phones.

(*The Times*, 23 June 2003)

All pronounce the point as though they think they are being original. In fact, the argument, together with the examples, seems to have travelled from person to person almost as a job lot. Thus among the discoveries and inventions listed in support of the argument that new technology is beneficial and resistance to it misguided, we find:

Lord May: *Galileo's work, vaccination, automobiles*
Blair: *Galileo's work, vaccination, lightning conductors*
Unilever chairman: *Galileo's work*
Scientists: *artificial insemination, vaccination, pasteurisation*
Stott: *DVDs, antibiotics, dentistry, vaccination*
Burke: *railways, the internal combustion engine, vaccination, antibiotics, mobile phones*

Certain examples recur, notably vaccination and Galileo's work. Others, such as automobiles and mobile phones, are rather odd, given general concern about their adverse as well as beneficial consequences. The examples are also highly selective. Noticeably, nobody mentions technologies – such as DDT, napalm, thalidomide, gunpowder, nuclear weapons – which humanity would have done better without.

On the surface, the journalistic use of language, in both broadsheets and tabloids, is very obviously unlike that of either politicians or scientists. It differs of course – as any carefully written language is likely to do – from unscripted talk in interviews. But in its lightness of touch and eye for entertainment it is also markedly different – though it shares their professional skill with language – from the speeches by Blair and May, and the proclamation by Bush. In terms of the triangle of communication this can be explained by the relation between speaker and hearer. Bush, Blair, May (and Charles) do not need to capture and keep the attention of the audience. We listen to their words because of their power and influence. Though newspapers also exert power, it is not of the same kind, and journalists must use words that will keep both their jobs and their readers' attention. The result is a greater focus upon the words themselves – on the centre of the triangle or on the window pane – which makes us more aware of how language is used ('Meacher the preacher', 'top banana') than of what is being said. This focus upon language itself is also intensified by the fact that very often the article is about what someone else has said. It is talking about talking. Yet despite these apparent differences, there are themes in these articles which echo and repeat some of the more ponderous arguments we have already heard.

In the next chapter, we look at a communicative situation which is different again: the language used by commercial companies. Unlike their consumption of newspapers, people do not choose their super-markets, nor do farmers buy their seed, entirely because of words. Nevertheless, words play their part, and a good deal of effort is put into courtship of the customer, which is not entirely unlike that of the reader by journalists or the voter by politicians.

4

COMPANIES

Food is business. Those who produce and sell it – seed companies, farmers, shops and restaurants – are inevitably major players in the GM debate, with those whose profits are the biggest tending to have the most to say. In this chapter we look at the pronouncements of supermarkets and biotech seed companies. Their voices, and their attitudes to GM food, are rather different. For while the biotech companies are almost by definition pro-GM, the supermarkets are more flexible, prepared to be blown, pollen-like, in whatever direction the winds may take them.

Supermarkets

We shall look at the supermarkets first. The strongest winds directing their policy are the obvious ones: profit, supply, demand and legislation. In some countries, this does not create any particular problem as far as GM is concerned. The USA and Canada have a plentiful supply of GM crops, no widespread public opposition to them, and no requirement for labels to specify GM ingredients. Consequently, GM food retail has been both profitable and unproblematic. Opposition to GM has been marginal and ineffective, emerging too late, after GM produce was already widespread. Thus, despite their general show of sensitivity to consumer opinion, and their extensive statements on matters of public concern, the web pages of the big US and Canadian supermarkets do not usually carry policy statements on GM.

In Europe, however, the situation is very different. An initial public outcry in the 1990s led to a moratorium on the growing of GM crops. Strict food-labelling laws insist that GM ingredients are listed. In Britain, supermarkets have responded to public disquiet by presenting a public face of concern about GM, by making their own brands 'GM free', and by removing GM products and ingredients from their shelves. More importantly from our point of view, they have produced a lot of words about GM, reflecting a general tendency to voice extensive opinions on any controversy even remotely related to their goods. At the time of writing, for example, the Tesco position on GM[1] appears among policy statements on recycling, mobile phones, carrier bags, packaging, climate change, emissions, refrigeration, transport, biodiversity and sustainable fisheries and forests. The modern equivalent of the garrulous greengrocer!

Yet despite this supermarket addiction to expressing opinions, issuing a policy statement on GM is by no means easy. The situation for European supermarkets is very tangled. Research findings, regulations and public opinion are constantly changing. Courting one market may alienate another. There are pressures from both consumers and suppliers.

Even for 'GM free' supermarkets like Iceland, which have sided against the new technology and banned all GM produce from their shelves, the task is by no means straightforward. Whether a product contains GM ingredients is not always clear. For while supermarkets may be reasonably confident about what goes into their own brand products, they cannot be so confident about the other brands they stock. For single-brand supermarkets this is relatively straightforward, and allows them to make a point at their competitors' expense:

> All Marks & Spencer food products are made without Genetically Modified ingredients or derivatives, and an increasing range of the animals we use in food production are fed on non-GM diets. As we sell only Marks & Spencer food, we can guarantee this, whereas the policy of retailers who sell different brands is sometimes out of their control.[2]

For others it is much harder. To track the history of every item sold is costly, time consuming and ultimately unreliable, making the supermarket vulnerable to revelation that it is not what it claims. As the Sainsbury's website puts it,

> The nature of the global trading market makes it difficult to identify a clear supply chain and therefore we could never guarantee that any of our products were GM-free. However, we are aware of customer concerns and we are reviewing this.[3]

Then there is the issue of traces of GM even in non-GM products. Even the most stringent labelling laws recognise that it is never possible to be sure that any item is 100 per cent what it says on the label, and therefore allow acceptable thresholds of contamination. As one supermarket web page ruefully points out,

> Setting such tolerance levels is normal practice. For example, in the case of durum wheat used in high quality pasta, the maximum level of other wheat permitted is 3 per cent and for organic, the maximum permitted level of non-organic material is 5 per cent.[4]

If we now look back at the Marks & Spencer statement – apparently so unequivocal – in the light of this impossibility, we see that the carefully phrased claim that Marks & Spencer food products 'are made without Genetically Modified ingredients' is not quite the same as saying that they definitely contain absolutely no traces of such ingredients.

Then there is the issue of foods which are not GM themselves, but whose production has nevertheless involved GM organisms. These include cheeses made using the GM enzyme chymosin in place of rennet, and meat from animals fed on GM fodder. A claim that food products are made 'without Genetically Modified ingredients' remains true in both of these cases, as neither the GM enzyme nor GM fodder are strictly speaking 'ingredients'. Though Marks & Spencer have nothing to say about cheese in the quotation above, they do tackle the GM fodder issue, saying that 'an increasing range of the animals we use in food production are fed on non-GM diets'. But 'an increasing range of animals' is not the same as 'all the animals we use'. And 'an increasing *range* of animals' (my emphasis) is not the same as 'an increasing *number* of animals' or 'an increasing *proportion* of the animals we use'. If we are told that something is increasing, moreover, we might wish to know by exactly how much.

Then there are the non-food GM products sold in supermarkets, such as clothes made from GM cotton. This is presumably why Marks & Spencer has to qualify carefully its claim, saying only that it is 'Marks & Spencer *food* products' (my emphasis) rather than 'Marks & Spencer products' that are 'made without Genetically Modified ingredients or derivatives'.

Given all these complications, those who are not well informed about the details of GM might well come to believe that the produce in a store is GM free when it is not. This complexity is aggravated by the attention supermarkets receive. As the battlegrounds in which the future of the GM debate may ultimately be decided, they and their policy statements are kept under close scrutiny by all concerned: regulatory bodies, consumer groups, the press, environmentalists and the biotech companies. So it is a difficult situation for them. Every word is watched and must be carefully chosen. This gives rise to convoluted attempts to be factually correct without alienating any potential market, attempts which could appear – were the implications not so momentous – positively comic.

Let us look in more detail at one statement: by the Co-operative supermarket entitled 'Food and genetic modification'.[5] It begins with a single-sentence paragraph: 'Most people don't understand what genetically modified food is, even though foods containing genetically modified ingredients are already on the supermarket shelves.'

This is a strange beginning, disconcertingly hard to pick apart. The document seems to start off in a conversational tone: 'most people' is rather vague, 'don't' rather chatty, and the grammatical structure 'most x don't x what x is' colloquial rather than scientific or legal. In this, the web page displays a typical characteristic of contemporary commercial discourse, referred to by the discourse analyst Norman Fairclough as 'synthetic personalisation':[6] a seeming familiarity with people who are in fact strangers which may make us less demanding in our interpretation of what is being said. We might not notice, for example, that the nature of the evidence that 'most people don't understand what GM food is' is not given. Nor, precisely, is it clear what it means to 'understand what genetically modified food is'. There are many different degrees and kinds of understanding, surely.

The next single-sentence paragraph is: 'Before they can be grown or marketed, experts must agree they are safe, but some people feel uneasy about "tampering with nature", while others, for religious or ethical reasons, would wish to avoid such foods.'

This implies, but also glosses over, an awful lot. It seems to suggest that legislation follows expert endorsement in a straightforward way. Once 'experts . . . agree they are safe', then GM ingredients can be 'grown or marketed'. But it does not say who the experts are, or how they are defined, what degree of agreement there has to be between them, or what happens if their opinion is divided. We are not told whether 'safe' means for health or for the environment. Another curious aspect of this sentence is its use of 'but'. Although the phrasing of the first part of the sentence carefully avoids saying that experts do actually agree, the use of this conjunction would make more sense in a sentence claiming that they do. We can see this clearly by deleting the hedging words 'Before they can be grown or marketed . . . must' from the first part of the sentence, making it: 'Experts agree they are safe, but some people feel uneasy about "tampering with nature", while others, for religious or ethical reasons, would wish to avoid such foods.'

In addition, the sentence sets up two highly questionable oppositions. The first is between 'experts' and 'people [who] feel uneasy about "tampering with nature"'. The second is between 'people [who] feel uneasy' and 'others [with] religious and ethical reasons'. The implication is that there are three discrete groups of people:

- experts
- people who feel uneasy
- others with religious or ethical objections.

No experts, it seems, are uneasy about tampering with Nature, nor do they have ethical or religious objections. There are many other implications too. The phrase 'some people' implies that it is only a minority who feel that GM is unnatural. It is also a phrase which, despite its apparently neutral meaning, can be shown by language corpus analysis (see Chapter 1) to have a generally negative prosody. That is, it is very often used when the people it refers to are being criticised. The phrase 'feel uneasy', moreover, suggests that their response is vague and emotional rather than clear and rational. The scare quotation marks around 'tampering with nature' suggest that genetic modification is not *really* tampering with Nature.

It is easy to let the chatty tone of this opening distract us from such matters, and it can seem churlish, faced with something so friendly, to subject it to this kind of rigorous analysis. The demands I am making for evidence, precise definitions and logical links seem to be overkill. Yet despite its disarming beginning, this document quickly becomes much more legalistic.

The conversational tone is maintained by a question and answer format which gives the impression that the supermarket is, in a casual and interactive manner, answering customers' questions, although these are in fact just as much the writers' contribution as the answers. (We have already seen this beguiling technique deployed in the article by Prince Charles, pp. 19–21.) Yet beneath this friendly wording lies great care never to claim that non-Co-op brands are GM free: understandably so, as for the reasons given above, the supermarket simply cannot be certain. Thus we have:

Do Co-op products use genetic modification?
For Co-op Brand products we have told our suppliers not to use genetically modified ingredients, but to use alternatives from separated sources. . . .

Other brands
Many major brands have also said they will eliminate genetically modified ingredients from their products. We have asked each of our suppliers what their policy is. If you ring the Careline we will tell you what they have said.

This is very carefully phrased. We are told what the Co-op has asked its suppliers to do, but not whether they have agreed. We are told that '*Many* major brands have . . . said they will eliminate GM ingredients'. But we are not told which major brands, how many of them, or whether they actually have done what they said. '*Major* brands', moreover, is a rather fuzzy category, as it is not clear where the dividing line is between major and minor. (An incidental implication is that '*minor* brands' have not made the same undertaking.) Lastly, any reader who might want to know more is diverted elsewhere. Interestingly, when I did ring the 'Careline', the young man I spoke to was not able to tell me what 'each of our suppliers . . . have said'. Indeed, he seemed understandably bemused by my question, pointing out politely that there were far too many suppliers to make a telephone answer to the question feasible.

In the latter parts of the document, despite the question and answer format, the legal tone gradually replaces the conversational one:

If food is not wrapped when sold, even if you buy it in a cafe or restaurant, you are still entitled to know if it contains genetically modified ingredients. From 19th September 1999 this information must be made available. . . .

What about trace levels?
In line with our campaign for honest labelling the Co-op will not label its products 'GM Free' even though we are aiming for zero levels of GM material in our own brand food.

We are specifying to our suppliers that they should use materials from identity preserved sources which enable the ingredient to be traced back to non-GM crops. However, we reluctantly have to agree with the Food Commission that it is probably now impossible to guarantee that minute traces of GM will not enter the food chain.

In order to protect consumers the EU has set a maximum level of 1% where non-GM sources are used. The Co-op believes the level should be as low as possible – 0.01% has been suggested as achievable for finished products.

And so on.

When they speak of GM, supermarket web pages are characterised by this skilful merger of the conversational and the legal, the general and the precise. On the one hand, they are lucid and easy to read. On the other, if approached with a lawyer's toothcomb, they say nothing either untrue or illegal. Yet for the casual reader, disarmed by the chatty style and trusting this wise adviser, there is a great deal which can be easily missed or misunderstood – usually to the supermarket's advantage. The effect suggests that a great deal of care and effort has gone into their preparation. Why such an investment of time and skill? One reason is perhaps that supermarket web pages are the major way for the store to publicise its views. Visitors are presumably already customers who, having chosen a particular store, are already well disposed towards it. Hardly surprisingly, the web pages receive large numbers of hits. They contain, after all, a lot of useful and enjoyable information concerning new products, bargains, cookery tips, competitions and so on, as well as – increasingly – facilities for on-line shopping. Even those who are not primarily interested in more serious aspects of store policy such as GM may stray into these areas through web pages.

Biotech companies[7]

When we come to the web pages of the biotech companies, however, both the content and the use of language are very different indeed. Here there is none of the light but precise style of the supermarkets. Instead we find acres of ponderous prose, as dull as a GM field, stretching for miles, much of it containing little information. Where the supermarkets distract us from the facts by their chattiness, the biotech companies send us to sleep with a sermon.

Here the question to ask is the opposite one. Why, given that the stakes are so high, do the biotech companies not produce the same kind of beguiling PR as the supermarkets? Part of the explanation is perhaps that their web pages are opened less frequently, and when they are it is for very different motives. There are far fewer reasons to visit a biotech company website than a supermarket one, and though they may be visited by shareholders, customers or employees, or even occasionally by people with some general interest in agriculture, much more likely are visits from journalists, corporation watchers or opponents of GM, searching for evidence. Perhaps that is one of the reasons why the function of the biotech companies' web pages seems to be more ritualistic and symbolic than genuinely communicative, and why an endemic vagueness has crept into their language. Unlike the supermarket websites, however, where it is interpretation which tends to be imprecise, in this case the confusion seems to emanate more from the writer than the reader.

Let us look at a concrete example. 'Welcome to Monsanto', began one version[8] of the company's web page: 'We are a global company committed to opening new doors that can help farmers around the world produce more and better food, care for their land and help protect the environment.'

To embody this message of goodwill, the web page showed a girl with blonde plaits and dungarees opening a door on to a sunny field of GM maize which stretches away in neat rows towards the horizon.[9] Although there have been numerous versions of the Monsanto message, a good deal of their web pages has been taken up with descriptions of the five-part Monsanto 'Pledge', refined and reworded over the years.

> The Pledge represents our stake-in-the-ground. It shows what we stand for as a company. It confirms our commitment as capable stewards of the technologies we develop, addressing tough issues honestly and openly, and delivering on values-based as well as science-based commitments.[10]

The five 'Pledge commitments' are:

- dialogue
- transparency
- respect
- sharing
- delivering benefits.

In the 2000–1 report 'Fulfilling our Pledge' the first of these is amplified as follows: 'We will listen carefully to diverse points of view and engage in thoughtful dialogue to broaden our understanding of issues in order to better address the needs and concerns of society.'[11]

This opening sentence stresses, rather as Prince Charles and Tony Blair both did, the importance of listening and dialogue, seen not just as ends in themselves but as a way to 'address the needs and concerns of society', as though one would lead directly to the other. But before we move on to consider this underlying faith in the automatic efficacy of dialogue, let us just pause to comment on the oddness of describing oneself as 'thoughtful'. It seems to violate a norm, rather as though someone were to say, not 'you are nice', which would be quite acceptable, but rather 'I am nice'. (Note also here the belittling characterisation, with which we are now quite familiar, of different points of view about GM as 'concerns'.)

Sociolinguists have terms for this norm, explaining it with reference to what they call 'A events' (ones of which the speaker has some privileged knowledge) and 'B events' (where the privileged knowledge belongs to the hearer).[12] Statements about A events refer, for example, to the speaker's own bodily sensations or emotions. Statements about B events might be evaluations by someone else. Thus it seems normal to say 'I feel ill' but not 'you feel ill', to say 'I like your haircut' but not 'you like my haircut' and so on. To describe in advance one's own engagement in dialogue as 'thoughtful' seems to be just such an abnormal evaluation.

Apart from this, the statement is very vague, and its implicit assumption that dialogue will automatically result in 'the needs and concerns of society' being addressed (presumably successfully) avoids the issues. Despite a widespread belief to the contrary (possibly originating in therapeutic practice), there is no reason why listening and dialogue should necessarily entail coming to an agreement.[13] It is at least equally likely, especially where there is substantial difference of opinion, that listening to the other side will deepen disagreement rather than mend it. This seems to be chronically the case in the GM debate, where however much the two sides converse, they have little impact on each other's perception. The steering committee on the 'GM nation?' public debate in Britain reported exactly this phenomenon. Only one-fifth of participants changed their opinion as a result of taking part.[14] In the study of people who began with only a mild opinion on GM, the trend was for participants to become more hardened in their views as they found out more about it.[15] Conversely, it is hard to imagine Monsanto abandoning GM technology as a result of listening and dialogue. The company presumably does listen to opposition groups, but only in the sense of 'listening in', monitoring opposition, just as the opposition in turn monitors them. In addition, any 'debate' or 'dialogue' can be exploited for market research: identifying the reasons for hostility to GM, and enabling companies to adjust their use of language accordingly.

The precise nature of 'the needs and concerns of society', so blandly referred to here, remains understood by the two sides in quite different ways. The phrase exemplifies a characteristic of corporate and institutional discourse with which we are all familiar: the use of evaluative terms without specific examples. Of course we will all agree that 'the needs and concerns of society' should be addressed, just as we want 'higher standards of public service', 'excellence in education', 'quality child care', 'justice for everyone' and so forth. But such statements, if not backed up with detail, tell us absolutely nothing. Even communists and capitalists can agree on the need for 'freedom and justice', atheists and believers on the importance of 'truth'. We may laugh about the excess of such generality in contemporary institutional discourse, but it constitutes a serious puzzle. If such statements carry no information, have no artistic merit, and if – as seems likely – nobody pays much attention to them, what are they for?

But perhaps there is more detail to come. The 2000–1 report tells us, in further amplification of the 'dialogue' Pledge, that

> We are accountable to a broad range of groups that give us license to operate: our shareholders, our customers, our communities, consumers, society, and each other. Accountability begins with taking ownership of our company's operations and success by being accountable for achieving results and making wise decisions. Accountability requires dialogue. Listening, consultation with customers and other important stakeholders, and involving outside views in internal decisions will help us to achieve the results that our shareholders expect.

The order of the list in the first sentence is revealing, and – to give Monsanto credit – honest. Shareholders come first. What is meant by 'our' in the phrases 'our shareholders' and 'our customers' is also clear. Its sense in the next phrase 'our communities', however, is ambiguous, as it could mean 'the communities we come from' or 'the communities which belong to us'. But what is meant by the quasi-legal phrase 'give us license to operate' and why is there no mention of 'governments' – the institutions which actually do license corporations? Is this perhaps the same as 'society'? If so, does 'society' refer to the whole world or only some parts of it? The last item in the list, 'each other', noble as the sentiment may sound, makes little sense. This becomes clear if we make it the only item: 'We [i.e. Monsanto] are accountable to . . . each other.' But if this is incoherent, the next sentence is even more so. 'Accountability begins with taking ownership of our company's operations and success by being accountable for achieving results and making wise decisions.' What can this mean? Are Monsanto not already owners of their own operations? 'Accountability' and 'being accountable' are the same thing, and so, pretty much, are 'success' and 'achieving results'. It seems circular, tautological and self-congratulating ('making wise decisions'). As far as I can disentangle it, the sentence seems to claim that taking ownership will lead to accountability, and accountability will lead to success. But what 'taking ownership' means, or why this should be the order of causes and effects, remains a mystery.

In the next sentence we are told, presumably in further justification of dialogue, that 'involving outside views in internal decisions will help us to achieve the results that our shareholders expect.' We are not told which outside views, and for obvious reasons. 'The results that our shareholders expect' must surely mean profits – and maintaining or increasing profits is incompatible with 'involving outside views in internal decisions' if these are views opposed to GM technology. So the only outside views which can be involved are those which support the company. The upshot of all this is that, for all its grand promises about 'listening' and 'involving outside views', Monsanto will continue to develop and sell GM seeds.

Writing my analysis of this paragraph has made me feel I am wading in treacle. I am a competent, educated native speaker of English, trained in the analysis of language. Yet when I look at these words, they do not seem to mean anything. They make sense only in a way so general as to evaporate into nothingness. And I fall into a trap of my own making, because in picking apart each convoluted proselytising sentence, I become guilty of the same sins myself: labouring the point, repetition, pedantic detail, verbosity.

What exactly is the problem? One is an absence of definition of terms, allowing them to be interpreted in different and partisan ways. Consider, for example, the words and phrases which seem to refer to groups of people.

we	our communities
diverse points of view	consumers
society	our company
a broad range of groups	other important stakeholders

our shareholders   outside views
our customers

Only two of these are precise (and also synonymous): 'our share-holders' and 'our company'. The rest seem vague and overlapping.

We have looked at one short extract in detail. The Pledge continues in the same vein. Here, for example, is part of a section on 'respect':[16]

> We will respect the religious, cultural, and ethical concerns of people throughout the world. We will act with integrity, courage, respect, candor, honesty, humility, and consistency. We will place our highest priority on the safety of our employees, the communities where we operate, our customers, consumers, and the environment.

Intent of the Respect element
The Respect element of the new Pledge goes to the heart of virtually everything that everyone at Monsanto does on a daily basis. It asks that Monsanto people build an awareness of the religious, cultural, and ethical philosophies of others into their thinking and that these issues be taken into account in their activities. This commitment can be understood as a simple common-sense approach to respect. In reality, without a deep commitment to respect, progress in the other four elements of the Pledge would be difficult so, in the end, progress on the Pledge as a whole will be one measure of commitment to the Respect element.

Nor is it only Monsanto that writes in this vague way. Here is an extract from the Syngenta Chairman and CEO:

> Our business is in an excellent position to help develop sustainable agriculture systems. We want to be a lively contributor to the debate on the best ways forward.
>
> This will be done in a spirit of openness and transparency as part of our everyday business. Our Code of Conduct guides every employee toward the highest standards of ethical behavior. Combined with our business performance, it is the foundation on which our reputation and our company will be built.
>
> We are profoundly conscious of the need to maintain an excellent health, safety and environmental performance,

while also dealing with the broader social issues associated with sustainable development.[17]

There is a notice about towels which must be familiar to anyone who stays in a contemporary hotel chain. One version I encountered read as follows: 'To help us to help the environment. We will only change towels which are left in the shower or on the floor.' Nobody can be taken in by this, and no hotel manager can be so silly as to suppose that they are. We all know that the real motive is to cut down on laundry bills. It can hardly even count as a serious attempt at deception – unless the author thinks the customers are fools. Yet such statements are endemic in official discourse.

How do we come to terms with them? We have become so used to corporate nonsense that it is all too easy to pass over it without paying it any attention. But is it right to do so? Surely language, like agriculture, should be used for better purposes.

Part II

THE SPOKEN ABOUT

5

SCIENCE AND LANGUAGE

Part I of this book discussed the categories of participants – the 'major players' or 'stakeholders' as they are called in the jargon: politicians, scientists, journalists and companies, with a chapter devoted to examples of the language of each in turn. There is one more category to come, notionally the most powerful in a democracy, and variously labelled, as in other topical debates, as 'the public', 'people', 'us', 'consumers', 'communities', whose views we shall consider briefly in Part III. In Part II of the book, however, our attention shifts from who is speaking to what is being said, and how linguistic choices lead us to see GM in particular ways. The purpose is to review the arguments and the language which we have already encountered, and try to dig beneath the surface foliage of words to uncover the roots of philosophical and political premises beneath.

As so much of the debate hinges on the relation between scientific and non-scientific language, this chapter returns to the issue of science, the way it is invoked in the debate, and some differences between scientific and everyday uses of language. The following two chapters discuss first (in Chapter 6) some key phrases used in arguments over GM and the values they reflect, and then (in Chapter 7) some of the metaphors and comparisons through which arguments for GM are expressed.

Appeals to 'science'

Perhaps the most deeply rooted premise is that the answers to all questions about GM food are to be found exclusively in 'sound science'. (Quite why 'science' needed the addition of this alliterative adjective 'sound' we shall consider later.) It is as though, once the scientific

evidence can be agreed, then the right decision will follow automatically. If it can be shown, in other words, that GM crops do have
adverse health or environmental effects, then they should be banned;
if not, then they should go ahead. One of the purposes of this chapter
and the next is to suggest that the relation between evidence and action
is more complex, and that the nature of this complexity can be eluci-
dated through careful examination of casually used words – including
the word 'science' itself.

People on both sides subscribe implicitly or explicitly to a simple
causal relation between scientific evidence and action. Thus, in British
politics, if we look at the apparently opposed views of Tony Blair and
Michael Meacher, we find this premise accepted by both. This con-
currence is explicitly acknowledged in the opening words of Michael
Meacher's most famous anti-GM article:

> At Prime Minister's Question Time in the Commons last
> Wednesday Tony Blair stated that 'it is important for the
> whole debate [on genetic modification] to be conducted on
> the basis of scientific evidence, not on the basis of prejudice'.
>   Exactly so. But what does the science actually indicate?
> Not I think what he appears to believe.
>
> (*Independent on Sunday*, 22 June 2003)

Thus, despite the obvious disagreements between these two antago-
nists, a rule of engagement is apparently agreed. It is, to extract Tony
Blair's words from within Michael Meacher's, 'for the whole debate to
be conducted on the basis of scientific evidence, not on the basis of
prejudice'.

In terms of the communicative triangle, then, the two adopt the
same stance towards the subject matter and expect others to do the
same. But let us look at this more carefully. It implies, very question-
ably, that there are two and *only two* possible criteria for decision-
making about GM, 'scientific evidence' and 'prejudice', and it thus
denies the validity of any other criteria. The most controversial word
in this agreed ground rule is surely 'whole'. Consideration of the
scientific evidence constitutes not 'a *part* of' but 'the *whole* debate'.
It is a shaky starting point for both sides. But Meacher is by no
means the only anti-GM campaigner, nor Blair the only GM advocate,
to present this view. We find it everywhere, and on both sides of the
debate. As a Monsanto representative put it to us, 'the one sort of truth
that you can try to stick to is the science'. Note that he said not 'one
sort of truth' but '*the* one sort of truth'.

To question these assumptions is to be on dangerous ground and open to easy misrepresentation, but it is exactly here that the pleas for rational, careful argument, so eloquently made by leading scientists such as Lord May (see Chapter 2), need to be taken seriously. To say that there are dimensions of the debate which are not scientific is neither necessarily to dismiss scientific evidence nor to succumb to irrationality and prejudice. Nobody involved questions the importance of scientific findings, or that, if there is evidence of harm or even of substantial risk of harm, as there appears to be,[1] then this constitutes a reason not to proceed with GM. But it is not a corollary that scientific evidence is *all* that is needed, 'the *whole* debate'. There may also be moral, political, social, psychological and aesthetic[2] reasons either to proceed or not to proceed with GM. In such areas, value judgements are needed, and it is this which places them beyond the pale of scientific enquiry. Not to acknowledge this distinction is the real betrayal of 'the values of the Enlightenment'.

Constant and exclusive appeal to science can distract us from the fact that behind the differences of opinion over the scientific evidence lie much deeper differences of values such that, even if the facts could be agreed, there would still be disagreement over what policy to adopt. The values in question concern three issues in particular: the natural world, social goals and political decision-making – all of which we shall turn to in due course.

But before we turn to the conflicts of value underlying key phrases in the debate, it will be helpful to consider some of the problems which are inherent, and perhaps ultimately inescapable, in the use of language to talk about science. There are aspects of meaning in everyday language which, unless rigorously resisted, can make what purports to be scientific entail kinds of meaning which are not. Although inevitable to some degree, this confusion can be combated, even if not completely eliminated, when there is a will to do so. Yet in the GM debate, as I think we have already seen, not only is this confusion not resisted by many of those claiming to speak with the authority of science, it is even courted and exploited. To make this argument clearer, and before moving on to consider how certain key words and phrases are used in the debate, I shall need to say something about science, something about language, and something about the relationship between the two. Though this will involve us in something of a digression, it is an important one. If the debate were to be – as Blair and Meacher demand – *wholly* scientific, then language would need to be used *only* in ways appropriate to science. When we turn to particular words and images in Chapters 6 and 7, my aim is to show that this is not the case.

The issue of scientific language is a large one, and a great deal has been written about it.[3] We shall confine ourselves to one of its simpler aspects: some of the ways in which the use and definition of words can differ in scientific and everyday language. Much could be also be said about other aspects of language use such as the grammar and the generic structures of scientific writing – but the examples here will serve, I hope, to make the main points.

Our focus is less upon communication between scientists (i.e. academic scientific language use) than upon references to science in other fora, including those, discussed in Part I, of politics, the media and business. The concern, in other words, is with appeals to science rather than science itself – and there are very many in the GM debate – or interventions by scientists in areas outside science. These reflect a common contemporary supposition that when a scientist speaks, in whatever forum, on whatever topic, and in whatever style, something of his or her authority carries over into these other domains. In this way, science has come to be seen less as a way of proceeding or as a mode of thought, and more as the property of particular people. There is a whole genre of popular books by scientists in which science is interwoven with non-science. Thus Richard Dawkins (to cite one of the best-known examples) is prone to lace his eloquent and informative accounts of scientific knowledge with, for example, discussions of religion, education and politics.[4] And even when discussing scientific findings, he uses techniques of explanation, such as the anthropomorphic personification of genes as 'selfish',[5] which are anything but scientific.[6] If the debate is to be scientific, a more rigorous dividing line is needed than has become usual between scientific and non-scientific uses of language. Let us look further into what might be involved.

The scope of science

Science is not easily defined. Yet there is some general agreement both about *what* it studies and *how* it does so, and therefore also about the kind of things it is *not* concerned with and the kind of methods it does *not* use. Let me try to summarise what seems to be agreed.[7] Science is concerned with understanding the material world in a process of constant dynamic interaction between theory and evidence, in which theories derived from rational consideration of the available facts are tested against further observation and experiment. All theories are provisional, however, and must be clearly stated in a way which can be challenged and falsified by counter-evidence and counter-argument. This entails in turn that terms must be precisely defined and claims clearly stated. The key points are thus the exclusive dependence upon rational argument and empirical evidence, and the openness to contestation. To be scientific, in other words, theories cannot be based merely upon assertion or intuition, nor can they be determined by aesthetic or moral evaluation, commercial expediency or the prevailing majority opinion. Science, moreover, aspires to be disinterested, driven by the search for greater truth, rather than, for example, by material gain or popularity (though it may on occasion also lead to both).

A relevant distinction, though one which is now seldom invoked in the GM debate,[8] is that between 'science' and 'technology', the latter being the application of a scientific understanding, whether for general good, for commercial gain or for military power. Though this is a crucial distinction, its virtual absence from arguments for GM strangely attracts little comment or concern, allowing proponents to position opponents as 'anti-science' rather than against one particular technology.

The dividing line has always been blurred, though more validly in some areas than in others. In medical research, for example, it would be ethically unthinkable to study the health of the human body without also applying that knowledge, while conversely the quest for understanding of the human body has generally been driven by its potential to prolong life and alleviate suffering. Medical science and medical technology, in other words, go hand in hand, though for moral rather than scientific reasons. Yet in other areas – and plant genetics is surely one of them – the relationship between the acquisition and use of knowledge is by no means so straightforward. Just as an understanding of energy sources need not necessarily lead to the development of transport or power generation, or an understanding of lasers necessarily to their use in weapons or in manufacture, so an understanding of plant genetics need not necessarily imply the development of GM agriculture.

Arguably, this distinction between science and technology is today more needed and more relevant than ever. Yet in recent years it has fallen by the wayside, and I have spoken to scientists who have swept it aside as hopelessly *passé*. The reasons are clear enough. As state-of-the-art science becomes ever more dependent upon government and industry for funding, and both of these sources increasingly demand only 'useful research' (with 'usefulness' interpreted only in particular ways), so science, rather than being a resource on which technology can draw, instead becomes driven by it, and the distinction disappears. With the demise of the distinction, the terms 'GM science' and 'GM technology' are used interchangeably by both sides in the debate. Indeed, the very phrase 'genetic modification' indicates the depth of the confusion, for the word 'modification' (like its abandoned precursor, 'engineering') is inherently technological rather than scientific, referring to an activity rather than a field of knowledge. Properly speaking, the science should be called 'plant genetics', and only the technology 'genetic modification'. This neglected point is crucial in untangling the arguments over GM. If we maintain the science/ technology distinction, it remains perfectly possible to be an opponent of GM technology without being an opponent of genetic science.

If we can maintain the distinction, then science, as opposed to technology, should be able first to give a clear account of what is involved in GM, and second to provide provisional theories of what its material consequences will be. It will not be directly concerned with other kinds of consequences in the realms of politics, commerce, ethics, economics and aesthetics – though those who do express opinions in these other realms may well draw upon science for evidence and information.

Words and meanings

Science aspires to define its objects of study with precision, to avoid ambiguity and vagueness, to confine itself to facts rather than evaluation. In many ways these aspirations are at odds with the nature of everyday language use which is inherently imprecise and evaluative, suited to types of meaning other than the scientific. There are thus many pitfalls inherent in the whole notion of 'scientific language', for words, to a lesser extent than formulae, are inherently slippery – notoriously so in the genres of politics, journalism and commerce.

Feature analysis and prototypes

Let us begin with what at first glance may seem straightforward: using words to refer to some objectively identified physical phenomenon, and categorising it as belonging to a precisely defined class. One way of doing this, which could be regarded as compatible with a scientific approach, is to have a checklist of verifiable characteristics, such that, if an instance has all of them, it must be an instance of that class. The word 'boy', for example, means 'male, juvenile, human being', and any entity which has these three characteristics is necessarily a 'boy'. But there are problems even with such an apparently straightforward definition, and its use to describe an actual state of affairs in the world: 'There is a boy at the front door' or some such statement. If the person at the door is an eight-year-old male, the situation is reasonably straightforward. But what if he is a seventeen-year-old? There might in that case be reason to say 'There is a young man at the door', depending on the role he is playing, whether he is within earshot, the speaker's own age and cultural background, and so on and so forth. Even apparently straightforward words like 'boy' are inherently tied up with indeterminate and intermediate instances, and with social contexts.

To deal with the problems of 'fuzzy' instances on the borderlines between categories (like the seventeen-year-old boy) semanticists have adopted a notion of 'prototypical' rather than 'absolute' membership, based upon psychological experiments on word recognition and production by Eleanor Rosch in the 1970s.[9] Thus a robin was found to be a more prototypical bird than an owl; a 'table' to be a more prototypical piece of furniture than a 'hat stand' and so on. In the case of 'boy', we could say that an eight-year-old would be a more prototypical boy than a seventeen-year-old, and a forty-year-old would be a more prototypical man. All this of course is subject to considerable cultural and contextual variation, and prototypical instances will differ with where and when one lives. The prototypical bird in Rosch's findings was actually an American robin (*Turdus migratorius*), reflecting the fact that the experiments were conducted in North America. For Europeans it might have been a blackbird (*Turdus merula*), for people in some parts of Africa a red-billed quelea (*Quelea quelea*). But the point is that this notion of some birds being 'birdier' than others, depending on where you come from, though it works in language and thought, has nothing to do with science, for which all of these, and owls and ostriches, are equal representatives of the class.

So we have two ways of defining a word. The first is done by checking off a list of features in order to be precise about category membership, the second is done much more vaguely, by comparing a particular instance with a prototypical representation. This is not to say that there are no ambiguous, border-line or intermediate cases in science, nor that it is free of disputes over the principles for establishing taxonomies, but only that precise criteria enable clear identification of class members, non-members and doubtful cases – as well as disagreement with the criteria themselves. They are necessary in science, but at odds with how word meaning usually works.

All this makes it impossible to use everyday words scientifically, unless they are redefined. The word 'boy' might validly be used in a scientific paper, but only after some precise indication of its meaning. One might say, for example, that it will refer only to 'human males between three and sixteen years of age', thus ruling out the vagueness which the word has in ordinary conversation. But, in this case, although a word has been borrowed from everyday language, it no longer has quite the same sense. 'Boy' can still be used to describe a seventeen-year-old in the world at large, but not in the scientific paper. Similar conflicts of definition occur when language use is controlled by law. The wording used on food labels, for example, may need to meet legal definitions. While for shoppers the description 'free-range chickens' may conjure up hazy images of hens pecking around in the dust on idyllic farms (a prototypical free-range chicken), the term is legally defined (both in Europe and the USA) as applicable to chickens with access to the outside.[10] In the USA the label 'made with organic ingredients' means, contrary to what one might expect, that only 70 per cent of the ingredients must be organic. For a product to be truly organic the label must say '100 per cent' organic'[11] – though even then there will inevitably be traces of non-organic ingredients. The way that we talk varies with context. 'Water boils at 100° centigrade' is fine as a general statement, even though the actual temperature varies with altitude. The danger arises when the kinds of definition being used are unclear or mixed. In arguments for GM this seems to happen very frequently. When we come to examine key words in the next chapter – such as 'purity', 'contamination' and 'escape' – we shall see that they bring with them far more than their scientific meaning.

Denotations, reference, connotations and prosody

But the problem with using words scientifically does not end with these matters of 'denotation': the relationship between the word and a class of phenomena in the world. There is also the issue of 'reference': what a word indicates in actual use. Let us stick with our example of 'boy'. The problem is not just that there is no agreed border-line between 'boy' and 'man'. Even when the person in question is not on this borderline, we might still choose either word. We can address an eight-year-old as 'young man', refer to a group of forty-year-olds as having 'a boys' night out', or talk of First World War casualties as 'just boys' (implying a criticism perhaps) or, more jingoistically, as 'our boys' or 'gallant boys'. We can also use a word to refer to something outside the normal denotation. Someone might talk about a kitten as a 'boy', or say 'come on my boy' when referring to something as completely un-boy-like as, say, a wheel nut which will not unscrew. In all of these cases, the choice of word says something about the person speaking as well as the person (or thing) spoken about. Our choices between these alternatives are largely to do with 'connotations' (the associative and attitudinal resonances of a word). This is clear too in choices between synonyms: we might say 'lad' instead of 'boy', or 'guy', 'chap' or 'gentleman' instead of 'man'. In addition there is the phenomenon of 'semantic prosody' (discussed in Chapter 1) referring to the fact that some words are more likely to occur in positive than negative contexts or vice versa. 'Lad', for example, is often found in approving descriptions while 'boy', though often neutral or positive, can also be used in a derogatory manner. In apartheid South Africa 'boy' was used to refer to an adult black male servant.

Discourse dependence

In addition, particular words and expressions belong to certain types of discourse rather than others. 'Gentleman' might sit more easily in the service-speak of restaurants and shops than in other kinds of inter-action. We can see this clearly if we try to spell out the meaning relations between sets of words which apparently denote the same or related phenomena.

Take, for example, the following words denoting horses: 'stallion', 'mare', 'gelding', 'colt', 'filly', 'foal', 'steed', 'nag'. The first six can easily be classified and related using parameters of sex and age.[12] But 'steed' and 'nag', though they also denote types of horse, do not belong with this set. While the first six might validly be used in a stable inventory, both 'steed' and 'nag' would be singularly inappro-priate. 'Steed' belongs in romances and tales, and 'nag' in jocular colloquial speech. Or, closer to our immediate subject matter, consider: 'animal', 'plant', 'mammal', 'insect', 'bird', 'tree', 'flower', 'herb', 'bush', 'shrub', 'weed'. There are different ways of arranging these words hierarchically to show superordinate and subordinate terms. This is because some of these words occur in scientific taxonomies of life; others do not. 'Bush' and 'shrub' are gardening terms, and 'herb' belongs to cooking or traditional medicine. Neither they, nor 'weed' (a key term in discussion of GM), have a scientific definition. To complicate matters further, the same words can have different meanings in different discourses. Thus while in scientific discourse an 'insect' or 'bird' is a kind of 'animal', and 'tree' is a type of 'plant',[13] this is not so in ordinary conversation. Other than ironically, I would not in conversation describe the poplar tree in my garden as a large 'plant', or the clothes moths in my wardrobe as 'animals'.

Word choice signals the kind of discourse we are involved in, and with it the speaker's evaluative and descriptive criteria. Criteria of beauty, for example, do not apply in scientific discourse, but they do in gardening. If I describe that poplar tree as 'a plant' then I am in scientific mode, if I say how beautiful it is in spring I am in conversational mode, if I talk about the 'weeds' or 'shrubs' beneath it I am in gardening mode, and so on. Where there is a shift from one kind of terminology to another there is also a change of value; where there is mixing of the two there is often confusion. As we shall see in the following chapters, many words and images used in arguments for GM draw upon several discourses at once.

Word choices in the GM debate

One major purpose of this book is to show how, in the GM debate, even when participants believe they are being factual and scientific in what they say, their non-scientific value judgements are nevertheless still evident in their choice of words. Neither the meanings of words nor the choices between them are as objective as they seem. Unlike more scientific representations such as mathematical formulae, the words we choose do not allow neutrality. In writing about GM, I too have made, inevitably, choices between synonyms which reflect my values: saying, for example, 'agriculture' not 'the farming industry', 'humanity' not 'mankind', 'psychological' not 'spiritual', 'social' not 'community' and so forth.

Both sides are certainly aware of such issues. Greenpeace, for example, seeks to identify words and phrases with negative and positive impacts through focus groups (though not specifically related to GM).[14] On the pro-GM side, instances of conscious choices abound, and there is sensitivity to both connotation and discourse dependence, and in particular to differences between scientific and everyday uses of language. For example, one pro-GM 'communication guide to improving understanding'[15] writes:

> *Language*
> In the area of communication on science and technical issues, the use of very technical language is often counterproductive.

Scientific jargon, although accurate, can confuse and even alarm non-scientists, evoking negative reactions.

Food biotechnology needs to be discussed in everyday terms. It is important for people to understand that the technology is about seeds that are planted in the ground and that grow into plants just like any other plants. If normal everyday language is not used then it sends the message that the technology is about experiments undertaken just in the laboratory and it gives a false impression of food biotechnology.

The understanding and acceptance of any science or technology including food biotechnology can change dramatically depending on the language used.

It goes on to give a list of 'words to use' including: 'ancestors, better, choices, concern, discover, explore, heritage, natural, partners, quality, safety, and tradition'. Then it gives a list of 'words to lose' ('because they have been found to confuse people') including: 'alter, ambitious, chemical, exploit, genetically engineered, laboratory, manipulate, pesticides, proven, revolutionise, short-term, and technology.'

Another pro-GM discussion document, circulated in Britain, recommends the importance of saying 'GM technology' not 'genetic modification technology', 'developing world' not 'third world', 'British farmers' not 'British agriculture' and so on. Monsanto has shown itself on occasion to be sensitive to the nuances of language. Thus, according to Michael Grunwald,[16] it was keen for its insulator polychlorinate biphenyls (PCBs) to be described with the words 'does not appear to be carcinogenic' rather than 'slightly tumorigenic'. In the late 1980s, aware of the negative reactions to the word 'hormone', it abandoned the phrase 'bovine growth hormone'[17] in favour of 'bovine somatotrapin',[18] later abbreviated to BST. In 2003, it took legal action to stop Oakhurst dairy in Portland, Maine, from labelling its organic milk (in language ironically reminiscent of Monsanto's own!) with the words 'Our Farmers' Pledge: No Artificial Growth Hormones', arguing (unsuccessfully!) that this should be replaced with a label saying 'No significant difference has been shown between milk derived from rbST-treated and non rbST-treated cows'.[19]

Something of a linguistic victory has already been achieved by GM proponents in successfully changing the name of what the debate is about. 'Genetic engineering' has been replaced by 'genetic modification':[20] a shift which has generally been rather foolishly accepted by the opposition. The GM scientists and biotech industry representatives we interviewed were quite unanimous and explicit in their preference for the latter: sensibly so – for while the two phrases refer to the same activity, their connotations are very different. 'Genetic engineering' has resonances of a mechanical and impersonal intervention (perhaps echoing the discredited phrase 'social engineering'), while 'modification' suggests something much less intrusive – only a slight adjustment of what already exists. The subsequent abbreviation of 'genetic modification' to 'GM', while still referring literally to the same activity, further distracts attention from the reality of what is being done. For the replacement of a full name with initial letters is not merely a matter of communicative economy. It may also, as George Orwell pointed out in *Nineteen Eighty-Four*,[21] distract attention from what these initials stand for. The accepted use of the abbreviation 'GM' rather than the full form 'genetic modification' (let alone 'genetic engineering') may be a case in point.

Hooray words

In a book bemoaning the absence of logic in much public and personal debate, Jamie Whyte[22] refers critically to two categories of word which he styles 'hooray words' and 'boo words'. 'Hooray words' refer to concepts and goals with which everyone will agree, until one gets down to the detail.

> besides justice, there is peace, democracy, equality, and a host of other ideals that everyone embraces, whatever they believe these ideals to consist in.
> And then there are the boo words: murder, cruelty, selfishness etc. Everyone agrees that murder is wrong, no matter how much they disagree about which killings are murder.

The GM debate is full of both, and we have already encountered many examples: the Monsanto 'Pledge' (itself a hooray word unless it is legally defined) to 'dialogue, transparency, respect, sharing, benefits' and commitment to 'better food' and 'improved crops'. The equivocation in the use of these words is evident not only in a general sense, but more specifically when the detail of Monsanto's actions is examined. Commitment to dialogue does not sit easily with allegations that Monsanto has monitored anti-GM activity through anonymous emails,[23] exerted pressure on *Nature* to withdraw an article by Ignacio Chapela,[24] contacted the printer of a special 1998 issue of the *Ecologist* which highlighted 'Monsanto's track record of social and ecological irresponsibility, and . . . its readiness to intimidate and quash those ideas which conflict with its immediate interests',[25] or its 2002 conviction under Alabama law for 'suppression of the truth, nuisance, trespass, and outrage' in dumping PCBs.[26]

But the 'hooray word' phenomenon goes deeper than these readily identifiable instances. Any word, however rigorously defined and exemplified in some contexts, can become a hooray word through constant vague overuse in others. An instance is the word 'science' itself. A myth seems to have developed in arguments for GM that language is being used objectively and scientifically when it is not. At the heart of what purports to be scientific debate we find imprecisely defined terms, evaluative words and a constant slippage from scientific discourse into other realms. For those who truly believe that science is important, rather than just glibly saying so, this contamination should sound very loud alarm bells. The glib use of the term by politicians and industrialists disguises issues such as the distinction between science and technology, and whether science can maintain disinterested objectivity when under political and commercial pressure. Like another favourite hooray word 'democracy', the concept of what we mean by 'science', and whether we are living up to its stringent demands, needs constant critical review if it is to survive.

Science is concerned with understanding the material world. Many of the posited dangers of GM, such as negative impacts on health and biodiversity, are certainly material. Yet there are also other consequences which, though not material, are nonetheless very real. Any major technology brings with it both cultural and psychological change. (Communications technology such as computers and mobile phones provide obvious examples.[27]) Where farmland and food are concerned, such consequences are potentially enormous. Both are heavy with cultural symbolism, and both have immeasurably important functions in the private lives of individuals. Cultural and personal values are expressed and developed through such activities as rambling,[28] gardening and cooking. Images of cultivation and eating are central to literature, art and religion. Consequently, there are few areas of life in which major changes to agriculture and food do not reverberate. Yet the GM debate proceeds as though GM were a scientific issue only. Quantifying risks and benefits in material terms (economic, nutritional, environmental) is done by both sides as though that were 'the whole debate'.

Clearly, by providing information about physical consequences, science has a key role to play in decision-making about GM crops and food. Yet neither acknowledging the authority of science in general, nor acceptance of particular scientific findings about GM, leads in any automatic way to either its acceptance or rejection. There is still room for different evaluation of consequences, different degrees of caution in the assessment of risks and benefits, and different ways of weighing scientific findings against other social, political, ethical and aesthetic factors. Countless analogies could be made with other areas of decision-making in which scientific knowledge is a crucial but not the sole criterion. Science, for example, can tell us about the causes and effects of nuclear explosions, but not whether nations are right to stockpile nuclear weapons and say they will use them in certain circumstances. Science can statistically assess the risks of a particular medical treatment, but cannot decide whether to use it in a specific case – that will depend upon the individual patient's disposition towards risk-taking. Science can describe the appearance of plants, their compatibility with each other and their reactions to certain conditions, but cannot determine entirely which ones a gardener actually wants.

All of these analogies are reasonable as there is a common element running through them, namely the relationship between scientific and other factors in decision-making. Yet there are dangers in argument by analogy which are worth noting. Each choice of example gives a very different 'spin' to the problem. Which are GM crops more like: nuclear weapons, surgery or a choice of flowers? It is easy to allow features other than the ones which are strictly analogous to taint our impressions – and in persuasive rhetoric analogies are chosen for exactly this reason. If proponents are to be scientific, analogy must be treated with care, and only the shared characteristics allowed to carry over from one domain to another. As arguments for GM are characterised by a surfeit of argument by analogy – explored in the next two chapters – this is worth bearing constantly in mind.

6

KEY PHRASES

Bearing in mind the differences in the use of language inside and outside science, in this chapter we look at words, phrases and ideas which are frequently used but seldom scrutinised in arguments for GM.

'Improved'

The word 'improved'[1] is used routinely to describe GM crops and food. It takes us back to where we began: President Bush's proclamation. He uses forms of the word 'improve' five times in less than 500 words, including an assertion that: 'Consumers enjoy continual improvements to the quality and quantity of our Nation's food supply.'

Here are some more examples (my emphasis throughout). Monsanto CEO Hendrik Verfaillie has stated that: 'The Monsanto goal in sharing the data is to facilitate and encourage research to *improve* rice and related crops around the world, and we are excited that this goal is being realized.'[2]

One of the company's pledges is: 'We will share knowledge and technology to advance science and understanding, *improve* agriculture and the environment, *improve* subsistence crops, and help small-holder farmers in developing countries.'[3]

The Syngenta website states that: 'The introduction of herbicide-tolerant and insect-resistant crops has increased the seeds market value by allowing seed products to gain premiums due to their *improved* traits.'[4]

Mark Henderson, science correspondent for *The Times*, writes that: 'European GM policies, however, were jeopardising the prospects for *improved* agriculture in Africa and Asia' (11 June 2003). A GM scientist, in a letter to the *Guardian*, writes that: 'Foods must be systematically *improved*, using all of the modern tools available, including gene rearrangement' (1 July 2003).

Such uses beg the question by prejudging the issue which is supposed to be under discussion: whether or not GM is an improvement. 'Improvement' has no absolute sense, but can only be understood relative to some particular value or yardstick. What needs to be examined is what constitutes 'improvement' from the various perspectives of seed companies, farmers, retailers, cooks, shoppers and consumers; from a more general human perspective; and for non-human species – animals, birds, insects and plants.

One sense of 'improvement' in food production refers simply to an increase in 'yield' (itself an equivocal word[5]). If yields are increased by GM (and there are many who claim they are not[6]) then this is clearly potentially good for food supplies, as well as companies' and farmers' profits. More altruistically, it can be argued (and frequently is by the biotech companies) that increased food production may help alleviate food shortages with an indirect benefit to health: a claim which is hotly contested by opponents with evidence that the problem is distribution, not production.[7] Alternatively, 'improvement' can be defined from the retailers' point of view. Certainly some genetic modifications – extending storage or shelf life and seasonal availability, increasing the uniformity of fruit, and so on – make the retailers' job easier and profits higher. All of these claims can be measured reasonably straightforwardly and scientifically.

But when we come to the concept of 'improved' food from the consumer's point of view, the epithet becomes much trickier and more ambiguous. 'Improved' food is presumably 'good' food – indeed better than it used to be. One sense of 'good' food is that it is nutritious in an 'eat-your-greens' sort of way. In this sense, the terms refer to a 'goodness' which may indeed be objectively measured, and is not just a matter of the preferences or pleasures of the eater. Children who ask why they should eat their greens receive the answer 'because they're good for you', not 'because you like them'. 'Good food' and 'food which is good for us', in other words, are far from being necessarily the same – as we all know only too well. Golden rice, which is modified to contain more Vitamin A, is apparently 'good' in this sense of being 'good for' the people who eat it. In fact it was the divergence between the food which people liked (a vitamin-deficient rice) and the food which was beneficial to their health (a vitamin-providing rice) which created the need for extra vitamins in the first place. (See Appendix 1.)

But there are cases where the food 'improvement' argument does not seem to refer to measurable factors such as yield increase, retail advantages or increased nutrition, but rather to 'good food' in its usual, vaguer and more colloquial sense of 'food which people like'. In some sections of the food industry, this perception of 'good food' is nevertheless treated as absolute, measurable and universal – an idea which ignores variations in food preferences between different individuals, age groups, social classes and cultures. Thus GM fruit and vegetables are presented as 'flavour enhanced', and are guaranteed to be of a certain taste. Some quite bizarre changes have been proposed to make things more 'friendly', such as a GM onion which can be cut up without causing tears,[8] or strawberries which will ripen (as one GM scientist put it to me) in time for the Wimbledon tennis tournament. Here the assumptions are about what people like rather than what they need. In these cases, 'good food' is a matter of subjective evaluation,[9] about which science can have nothing to say. If it does, it has surely overstepped its mark and strayed – like a wind-blown seed – across the separation area which it has so carefully and correctly established around itself.

The notion of 'good food' well illustrates that human and environmental concerns cannot be kept apart. The focus-group research which Elisa Pieri, Peter Robbins and I carried out as part of our second research project[10] on the discourse of GM suggests that even if food were consistent, nutritious, plentiful and cheap, it would not necessarily feel 'good' if these qualities had been bought by turning an ecologically diverse countryside into spiritless monocultures, as illustrated by the following two exchanges (* indicates a change of speaker):

> * And if you go abroad . . . I've been to Lesbos and you see beautiful meadows there with natural . . . and the bird life is wonderful because the fields are full of poppies and all the wild flowers and they're absolutely stunning
> * It's untouched by pesticides
> * You come back and it's that sterile
> * That's right yes
>
> * Well I'd participate yes. I'm more again the organic. I want to go to the same study for the wildlife and the bees and everybody else, and get back to what it was in the 1940s and
> * Organic and farmers market
> * I mean at least you could walk out in the fields. You can hear all the different kinds of birds, and all the different

kinds of wildflowers in the hedgerows. I mean I'm sorry you people haven't seen it. You weren't born. But I mean you went out in the 30s and the 40s and the 50s and it was beautiful each farm.

'Sound science'

The phrase 'sound science' (and synonymous expressions such as Tony Blair's 'proper science') occurs quite frequently in the arguments of both sides. Here are some examples (my emphasis throughout). In 2003, the US State Department website carried a paper published by the business lobby group, the National Foreign Trade Council, entitled 'Looking behind the curtain: the growth of trade barriers that ignore *sound science*'.[11] In May 2003 Patrick Bateson, Vice-President and Biological Secretary of the Royal Society, said: 'The public have a right to decide whether they want to buy GM foods, and are entitled to have access to sensible and informed advice, based on *sound science*' (*The Times*, 8 May 2003). The 2000 Cartegena protocol,[12] an international agreement on GM, allowed governments to block GM imports only if their decision was based on '*sound science*'.[13]

Why does the noun 'science' need this qualifying adjective 'sound'? In a strict sense it seems superfluous and tautological: science must be sound if it is to be science at all. One of its main functions is perhaps to imply that there is also, in addition to 'sound science', other science which is 'unsound'. The rhetoricians of both sides who include this phrase in their harangues are not always explicit about what form this 'unsoundness' may take. Let us consider the possibilities.

Science might be unsound in the sense that, while genuinely trying to follow scientific principles, it is just full of mistakes: the methods are flawed, the evidence is wrong, or the calculations or inductions incorrect. This is the kind of allegation which is levelled by the pro-GM lobby against the work of those scientists who claim to have discovered negative effects, like Pusztai, Chapela or the Cornell team investigating the decline of monarch butterflies (see Appendix 1, pp. 136–7). It is levelled by the anti-GM lobby against experiments apparently disproving such effects. For example, an experiment[14] which claimed to prove that bovine growth hormone did not survive in pasteurised milk was described as flawed by Jeffrey Smith[15] on the grounds that the milk was boiled for 30 minutes instead of 60 seconds. According to the British government's Advisory Committee on Releases to the Environment,[16] some people consider that the favourable evaluation of the effects of GM maize on biodiversity in Britain was only made because the conventional maize crop used in the comparison had been sprayed with Atrazine, a particularly destructive chemical, already being phased out.

A different but related sense of 'unsound' science is one that suggests it has been bought by interested parties, whether government, industry or NGOs – that it betrays, in other words, the noble aspiration expressed by the Royal Society motto, *Nullius in verba*,[17] that science should serve no other interest than itself. Here the opponents of GM are on strong ground. For while those producing pro-GM findings are paid directly or indirectly by governments and companies, those whose findings support the anti-GM case have not generally reaped either financial or professional benefits, but have often found their personal position worsened as a result of their work. Thus whether or not they have made mistakes in their science, they have certainly not protected their own interests. This understandably lends their findings more credibility. Indeed, a disturbing fact for non-scientists trying to weigh up the evidence is that there are few, if any, scientists actively campaigning for GM food technology who are not directly or indirectly funded or salaried by the biotech industry or pro-GM governments. There are also many who have direct financial interests in biotech companies.[18] The problem here is again the contemporary failure to distinguish between science and technology, masking a reversal of the relation between the two. GM research is not conducted first for its own sake and then later, and in part, used as a basis for applications. Rather, it is driven by preconceived commercial applications and government policies.

A third sense in which science may be 'unsound' involves the way it relates – even if its findings are true – to other human activities and concerns. Science may be both correct and independent but still unacceptable on some other, extra-scientific, criteria – ethical, political or aesthetic. Here, too, a distinction between science and technology is needed, for it is usually the technology rather than the science itself which is undesirable. The technology of nuclear weapons – clearly based on correct science – is a case in point. Another, closer to the topic of GM, is DDT. The initial research, though scientifically correct, excluded consideration of its effects on wildlife.[19]

The phrase 'sound science' is not in itself very sound. When used by scientists it can become self-congratulatory (rather like Monsanto's 'thoughtful dialogue') and circular: an epithet awarded by those on one side of a scientific dispute to themselves, and denied to their opponents. Used by politicians and governments, it is reserved for the scientific evidence which supports their own policies.

Perhaps, too, its appeal to rhetoricians is more to do with its alliteration than its meaning.

'Frankenstein foods'

The memorable alliteration 'sound science' is certainly matched by the most famous GM phrase of all, 'Frankenstein foods', first used in the *Daily Mail* on 28 January 1999. Ironically, it is now used far more often by the pro-GM lobby than by the opposition, for whom it seems to have long since served its purpose. Proponents of GM use it to characterise what they see as the irrational nature of the opposition. Thus a corpus search of our data reveals it as most likely to occur in contexts such as the following, preceded by 'so-called' to express both disagreement and distance. Even without the full citations, they give a flavour of the way the phrase is used:

- 'Lurid warnings about "Frankenstein foods" have bedevilled the discussion'
- 'Fed a steady diet of Frankenstein food stories'
- 'All this talk of Frankenstein food is misleading'
- 'GM products have been dubbed Frankenstein foods over fears they could mutate'
- 'a debate more known for hysterical panic over "Frankenstein food"'
- 'unless he stopped questioning the safety of so-called Frankenstein food'
- 'As a result of growing fears over "Frankenstein foods", ministers agreed last summer'
- 'However, the fight against so-called Frankenstein foods will suffer a blow today'
- 'who are fearful about the safety of so-called Frankenstein foods'.

In our interviews with GM scientists, the phrase was used to sum up all press coverage of GM. When we interviewed Ian Gibson MP, Chair of the Parliamentary Office of Science and Technology, he used it no fewer than five times in half an hour as an example of language that is intended to sway opinion. It has become, it seems, a shorthand label to refer to irrational, uninformed, media-led resistance to GM.

In this sense, the phrase has rebounded upon those who first used it, and is now deployed, quite effectively, to brand and dismiss the opposition. Even opponents of GM, anxious to assert their scientific credentials, are noticeably wary of it. As with any frequently used phrase, it has lost some of its initial semantic resonance and is now referred to equally glibly by both sides.

Does it deserve this disdain? Does it have nothing to add to the debate? It is worth returning to its first use, asking what was meant and understood by it, and why it has exerted such an influence.

The phrase invokes two related but distinct ideas, reflecting the trajectory of the Frankenstein story itself. On the one hand, it draws upon Mary Shelley's novel *Frankenstein, or the Modern Prometheus*, first published in 1818,[20] about Victor Frankenstein, a brilliant scientist who claimed 'benevolent intentions, and thirsted for the moment when I should put them in practice'. The book tells how he created a 'creature' out of body parts, and gave it life with electricity. This artificial 'man', initially sensitive, intelligent and kind, finds himself rejected by everyone he meets. Frustrated and in need of love, he embarks on acts of violence and cruelty, eventually murdering Frankenstein's wife in revenge for his creator's refusal to make him a female companion, and retreating from humanity to the Arctic wastes. In this original version, the story is told through a series of concentric narratives: letters from an explorer named Walton, the account of Victor Frankenstein, and the narrative of the 'monster' himself. It is this innermost narrative which has ironically seemed to many readers both the most sympathetic and the most reliable, bringing a richer perspective on the events than the accounts by either scientist or explorer.

On the other hand, the phrase invokes the many subsequent adaptations of the novel, especially films. In these, the voice of Frankenstein's creation has been taken away. There is no interplay between his perspective and those of others. He has become simply a rampaging monster, violent and destructive from the outset. Thus while in the original novel he learns both to speak and to read and write,[21] even in the first adaptation for the stage[22] he was already mute, and so he has remained in the many horror-film versions that have followed. Evoking these film images (as it probably does for most readers), the phrase 'Frankenstein foods' suggests not so much the theme of irresponsibly applied science as a direct association between GM crops and the monster, dramatically personifying their potential to escape, cause damage, and go out of control. The image is perhaps of monstrous plants causing direct harm, perhaps with strangling tentacles. This was undoubtedly the image our interviewees believed the phrase conveyed. One 'non–expert' associated it with John Wyndham's *The Day of the Triffids*, a science-fiction novel about mobile and murdering plants brought to earth by meteorites. A less successful phrase, 'mutant crops', coined three weeks after 'Franken-stein foods' by another British daily, the *Express* (18 February 1999), also uses a word associated with horror films and was presumably intended to create something of the same effect.

'Frankenstein food' has become the 'F word' of the pro-GM lobby. Clearly, it has struck a nerve, whichever version of the story it evokes. But are the proponents of GM right to dismiss the fears which the association with the Frankenstein story expresses? Mary Shelley's story is one of scientific hubris, a quest for knowledge without con-sideration of human and social consequences, a disregard for indivi-duals and their feelings. The later adaptations, albeit more superficial and sensationalist, preserve some element of that myth, but concen-trate more upon the unforeseen physical consequences of uncontrolled experimentation. Perhaps what really irks the pro-GM lobby is the accuracy of the association, and its encapsulation in a memorable alliterative phrase.

'Interfering with Nature'

The notion of 'interfering with Nature' occurred quite frequently in our interviews and focus groups, even if not in these exact words. Other synonymous phrases, each with a somewhat different conno-tation, were:

fiddling around ⎫
interfering ⎪
meddling ⎪
playing ⎬ with Nature
tampering ⎪
tinkering ⎭

Yet although the notion is prominent in lay discussion of GM,[23] it seldom appears (other than to be mocked by pro-GM voices as hope-lessly romantic and primitive) in the institutionalised discussions of government, academia or industry, where 'Nature' has been replaced with 'biodiversity', a word whose lexical formation echoes that of 'biotechnology'. It would be all too easy to assume that they are synonymous and that 'Nature' is just the lay person's way of referring to 'biodiversity'. But this is not necessarily the case. 'Biodiversity' belongs to the discourse of science, while 'Nature' (notwithstand-ing the journal title *Nature*) belongs also to that of poetry, religion, recreation and personal discussion. Spelt with a capital letter, it evokes a personified 'Mother Nature'.[24] And although 'interfering with Nature' may be taken to refer to the same phenomenon as 'reducing biodiversity', it implies a quite different line of argument. Biodiversity can be quantified, but this quantification, whatever the findings, in itself makes no value judgement. Simply to say on scientific evidence, for example, that GM does or does not reduce biodiversity does not constitute an argument for or against it. For such statements to become arguments they need to be combined with evaluative criteria. When proponents of GM talk as though evaluation follows automatically from quantification, they fail to address the possibility that different people's evaluative criteria can be different and incompatible.

Another common objection to GM, invoking a word derived from 'Nature', is that it is not 'natural'. In discussions involving GM scientists, we repeatedly encountered the same argument against this popular view. This was that the word 'natural' cannot be precisely defined, that the borderline between the 'artificial' and the 'natural' is impossible to fix, that even traditional agriculture is 'unnatural', and that therefore the objection that GM is 'unnatural' is vapid and meaningless. This argument tended to be advanced with an air of triumph and finality (in a 'QED! I rest my case!' kind of way) as though the speaker had made a great discovery and had played a trump card against the opposition. But, as should be evident from the discussion in Chapter 5, it shows a deep misunderstanding of word meaning. Neither 'natural' nor 'unnatural' can be defined by a checklist of necessary features, but that is not to say that they have no meaning. They are words best understood by reference to prototypical instances. It makes sense to talk of degrees of naturalness, and to place different phenomena at different points along a continuum. Thus a plant growing in a wilderness is prototypically natural; a GM plant growing in a laboratory is considerably less so.

Attempts to use the term 'natural' precisely, on the other hand, to mean that which occurs in Nature and without human intervention, inevitably come to grief. As a report by the pro-GM Nuffield Council on Bioethics put it,

> The 'natural/unnatural' distinction is one of which few practising scientists can make much sense. Whatever occurs, whether in a field or a test tube, occurs as the result of natural processes, and can, in principle, be explained in terms of natural science.[25]

Despite its internal contradiction (saying first that the distinction between the words 'natural' and 'unnatural' makes no sense and then using one of them twice in the following sentence),[26] there is a reasonable point here: that the terms are not scientific. Yet the reason why they are out of place in scientific discourse is not only their imprecision. It is also because, in addition to describing a phenomenon, they also express a judgement. Saying that GM is natural or unnatural is not like saying that there is, or is not, water on Mars. But this is not to say that such statements are meaningless, any more than other utterances using evaluative, graded expressions, such as 'love' in 'John loves living in London', or 'brilliant' in 'It's a brilliant film.' It is just that, like those words, it does not belong in the realm of science.

The Nuffield Council on Bioethics had more to say on the topic in a later report,[27] supporting the use of GM crops in poorer countries. It introduces its discussion of whether GM is natural as follows: 'Some people think intuitively that it cannot be right to change the "essence" of natural objects like plants. Arguments about "naturalness" are complex, and raise many difficult issues.'[28] It does not tell us who these people are, or why the reporting verb 'think' is qualified with 'intuitively'. (Surely the opposite view would be no more or less intuitive.) In addition, the relation between the two sentences seems to imply a contrast between the simplistic arguments of 'some people' and the council's own more complex ones. And the scare quotes suggest that the concepts of essence and naturalness are invalid.

In its next paragraph the report elaborates its view of 'naturalness' as suspect:

> Conventional plant breeding is often understood as the selection of particular individuals from a great variety of naturally occurring types of plants. This activity tends to be seen as natural. Many would also view the systematic interbreeding of naturally occurring types of plants in the same vein. However, plant breeders also create plants which would not be achievable by judicious interbreeding, using techniques such as wide-crossing. This has led to completely new varieties such as Triticale (a hybrid between wheat and rye). Another technique, mutation breeding, involves the exposure of plants and seeds to radiation and chemical substances. These procedures have been, and still are being used to produce many important staple crops around the world. . . . Thus,

it is important to note that the deliberate alteration of plants as they occur in nature has been practised and accepted for several decades. In this context, genetic modification can be seen as a new means to achieve the same end; it is certainly used in that way. It differs from conventional plant breeding in that it can allow for much faster and more precise ways of producing improved crops. For this reason, we concluded in our 1999 Report that it was not helpful to classify a crop that has been arrived at by means of conventional plant breeding as 'natural', and to classify a crop with the same genetic complement as 'unnatural' if it has been produced through genetic modification.[29]

This paragraph does some strange things, and it is worth subjecting its reasoning and language to scrutiny. Its purpose seems to be to deny the validity of any 'unnatural/natural' distinction when applied to plants. Yet despite this, the first sentence itself uses the term 'naturally occurring', without the scare quotes it used for 'naturalness' in the paragraph before. Thus (like the earlier report) it *does* acknowledge in practice a distinction between 'natural' and 'unnatural'. However, unlike those opposed to GM as 'unnatural', it seeks to place the boundary between plants which occur without any human intervention and all plant varieties which occur through intervention of any kind. This implies that there is a discrete boundary between the natural and the unnatural.

Note, too, how the report sets up the views it opposes without being specific about whose views they are: 'This activity tends to be seen as natural. Many would also view the systematic interbreeding of naturally occurring types of plants in the same vein.' This is achieved first by the passive verb construction 'tends to be seen', which allows the agent (that is to say, the people who see) to remain unspecified, and second by the vague 'many'. In addition the verbs are heavily hedged – 'tends to be seen' rather than 'is seen'; 'would also view' rather than 'view' – as though these unnamed people are rather vague and impressionable, not quite sure of themselves. The link to the next sentence needs to be inferred: 'However, plant breeders also create plants which would not be achievable by judicious interbreeding, using techniques such as wide-crossing.'

Points which are suggested rather than stated explicitly are often more insidious as they are hard to pin down and easy to deny. Whereas a single sentence can often be judged for its truth and logicality, relations between sentences are often left unstated.[30] Here, the word 'however' seems to suggest that this sentence posits a counter-argument to the views reported in the two preceding sentences. It seems to assume that 'wide-crossing' is something which opponents, in their ignorance, are unaware of, as they will also be of 'mutation breeding' which 'involves the exposure of plants and seeds to radiation and chemical substances'. But from this point the logic of the paragraph seems to fall apart. Having presupposed that the 'natural/unnatural' distinction is discrete rather than graded (i.e. a question of 'either/or' rather than 'more or less'), and established four types of plant (naturally occurring, conventionally bred, wide bred, mutation bred), it now tells us that a fifth type, GM plants, 'can be seen as a new means to achieve the same end' as wide-breeding and mutation breeding, and that 'for this reason' it should not be classed as 'unnatural' in contrast to a crop which 'has been arrived at by means of conventional plant breeding'. But this – to put it mildly – begs the whole question. The fact that it may be a means to the same end is irrelevant to the issue of whether it is natural. (You may as well say that travelling in an aeroplane is as natural as walking because they are both means of moving.) All this paragraph does is to assert where its authors place the boundary, and then use this as a reason for discounting the views of others who place the boundary elsewhere. It is no more or less logical to say that these five types of plant are progressively less natural, or to place the boundary after wide-breeding. The conclusion is that it 'it [is] not helpful' to distinguish GM plants as 'unnatural'. But the word 'helpful' is meaningless if we do not specify for what purpose or to whom.

The cultural theorist Raymond Williams,[31] discussing the etymology and different senses of the word 'Nature', gives three related meanings and explores the ambiguous alternations between them.[32] The three senses are: '(i) the essential quality and character of something; (ii) the inherent force which directs either the world or human beings or both; (iii) the material world itself, taken as including or not including human beings.' A good deal of confusion arises from any discussion which does not recognise these different senses – the Nuffield Council discussion, for example, uses only sense (iii), 'taken as including human beings'. In addition, uses of both words – 'Nature' and 'natural' – draw more upon their connotations than their denotations. Corpus searches reveal that sense (iii) has a generally positive prosody (with the notable exception of the phrase 'natural disaster') indicating that – at least in modern times – people have a deep belief that Nature and what is natural tend to be good.

Though proponents of GM point to phenomena which are 'natural' and bad (two recurring favourites being viruses which can be combated through vaccination,[33] and potentially harmful fungal toxins on organic crops[34]) these have little impact on this widespread view that, all other things being equal, what is 'natural' is preferable to what is not. Even the pro-GM lobby, by rebutting charges that GM is 'unnatural', show at least partial acceptance of this belief.

Why should Nature and the 'natural' generally be regarded as good? The belief is founded, quite reasonably, on a perception of natural processes (in the sense of those which occur without human intervention) as predominantly life-giving and healing, reliable, and independent of human error and malice.

Progress and change

Many on the pro-GM side see such views as hopelessly romantic, impractical and flying in the face of progress. Their reasoning, however, is worth looking into carefully.

A conversation which Elisa Pieri and I had with one GM scientist took a curious but not untypical turn. He was explaining to us the benefits of GM over conventional intensive farming, claiming that it reduced the use of insecticides and herbicides. He made the usual assertion that his views were based on sound scientific evidence, and that this must be the only basis for decision-making. It was his expertise in the science, he implied, which made his views authoritative. As the comparison was only between conventional farming and GM agriculture, we asked why organic farming was not preferable to either of the other two. Without apparently registering any change of tack or contradiction in his argument, he answered that, if weeds were not removed by chemicals, an army of farm labourers would be needed, and this would reduce farming profits and was no longer feasible socially. Thus the argument shifted seamlessly and without hesitation from a scientific to an economic basis. His expertise as a scientist licensed him to speak as an expert economist. The point here is not whether he was right or wrong (though even his science is highly disputable), but how easily those who claim to argue only from scientific evidence change their grounds. Such shifts are common in the GM debate, as is the assumption that expertise in one area translates into expertise in others. Like seeds themselves, arguments in one bucket can in practice spill over into the next, and it is hard to keep either as pure and unadulterated as the scientists would like.

This raises the more general point that the application of GM technology will in practice be a matter of farm management rather than
science. Whatever may happen with chemicals in GM trials conducted
by scientists, there is no reason to suppose that the same would happen
on a real farm, in the hands of a farmer whose aim is not to make
measurements but to make a profit, and who has neither the time
nor the expertise to be precise. Such a farmer may well add 'just a
little bit more just to be sure' – rather as the scientists like to add a
little more to their arguments.

A very common shift of this kind in pro-GM arguments is from
assertions of the health or environmental safety of GM to an assertion
that it is 'progress'. 'Progress' is a classic hooray word. If it means
'change for the better', then of course everyone will be for it. But,
rather obviously, not all change is for the better. There are also changes
for the worse: in politics, the Nazi seizure of power, for example, or
the emergence of Stalin as Soviet leader; in technology, the development of nuclear weapons, or DDT, or thalidomide. No reasonable,
morally responsible person could be for change per se. The issue about
a new technology is not whether it brings change – it does that by
definition – but whether that change is good or bad.

Those against recent changes in agriculture (whether from traditional to intensive farming, or to GM crops) are frequently accused
of being against progress. Here for example is Niall FitzGerald, the
Chairman of Unilever.

> Agricultural practices and food processing have never been
> static. Our European forefathers made the switch to settled
> agriculture in the stone age. One wonders if there was a Neo-
> lithic George Monbiot – urging his clansmen to stick to the
> old pastoral ways and avoid this dangerous and potentially
> harmful innovation.
>
> Since that fundamental development our agriculture has
> been driven forwards by endless innovations: the plough, the
> watermill, plant breeding, the use of agricultural machinery,
> and now the prospect of biotechnology. There is no reason
> why change in the UK has to stop now. To cease to innovate
> is to accept stagnation and failure.[35]

Leaving aside some curious details – like the omission of poisonous
chemical sprays from the list of innovations, the emotive word 'fore-
fathers', and the failure to mention that agriculture began in the
Middle East – the message is clear, especially in the last sentence.

'Innovation', like 'progress', is a word denoting change, but one with a very positive prosody, and it sidesteps the key unanswered question: why are all changes being presented as progress? What is the *logic* of saying that because there were changes for the better before GM, *therefore* GM must also be good?

'Luddites'

Where there are hooray words like 'progress' and 'innovation', there are also boo words to refer to their opposites. A key boo word in arguments for GM is 'Luddite'.

Here are some examples. On 10 January 2003, US trade official Robert Zoellick described EU policies on GM as 'immoral', 'anti-scientific' – and 'Luddite'.[36] The official report on 'GM nation?', summarising arguments, says that 'they [people in favour of GM] directly attack opponents' concepts of caution, which (they say) would have prevented almost any advance in technology, including agriculture itself. The word Luddite is often used.'[37] It reports that 'opposition to the concept of precaution/Luddism' was one of the 'predominant themes' of letters and emails in support of GM.[38] One of the scientists we interviewed described protestors as 'crop-tramplers with a Luddite agenda' in contrast to 'lay people with a general curiosity'. The former US Secretary of Agriculture Dan Glickman, who became openly disenchanted with the Clinton administration's pro-GM policies, summed up the use of the word as follows:

> What I saw generically on the pro-biotech side was the atti-
> tude that technology was good, and that it was almost
> immoral to say that it wasn't good, because it was going to
> solve the problems of the human race and feed the hungry
> and clothe the naked. . . . And there was a lot of money
> that had been invested in this, and if you're against it,
> you're Luddites, you're stupid. That frankly was the side
> our government was on.[39]

Even when the actual word is not used, the stance it signifies – mindless and violent opposition to any new technology – is frequently invoked. Jack Kemp, a former Republican nominee for Vice-President, described opponents of GM as 'ill-considered, anti-progress, left-wing, self-appointed . . . anti-technology activists'.[40]

'Luddite' has come to mean anyone irrationally opposed to new technology. But let us, as with 'Frankenstein foods', return to its origin. The original Luddites were early nineteenth-century weavers in the English Midlands who protested against the introduction of the 'wide frame' loom, sometimes by destroying the new machines. Although popular wisdom has caricatured them as dim-witted, thuggish and badly organised, there is no historical reason to attribute any of these characteristics to them.[41] Their protests were not against the machines themselves, but rather the new pricing system introduced with them and the effect upon their own livelihoods. Contemporary accounts of Luddite raids on workshops describe how only the frames of owners following the new pricing system were smashed, while others were left untouched. And they were well organised, striking selectively and effectively in groups of up to 100 men. As for the charge of disproportionate violence, it applies more to the authorities than the protestors. In response to the popularity of the movement, the destruction of machines was made a capital offence – for which seventeen Luddites were executed in 1813. In short, the Luddites were not themselves 'Luddite' in the sense in which the word is now used. The term says more about those who use it than those to whom it is applied. As Kirkpatrick Sale puts it in his revision of the usual account: 'They were rebels against the future that was being assigned to them by the new political economy taking hold in Britain, in which . . . those who controlled capital were able to do almost anything they wished.'[42]

But there is a twist to the contemporary use of 'Luddite' to describe opposition to GM. US trade official Zoellick (quoted on p. 105) went on to say of Europe that its 'anti scientific' policies were spreading to the developing world and convincing famine-hit countries to refuse GM food aid. So the contemporary Luddites are rather different from the original ones. They are not the poor and oppressed, but the rich oppressor. This shades into another common pro-GM characterisation of those with anti-GM views – that they have the luxury of holding them only because they have the privilege of a rich northern lifestyle. As one pro-GM voice expressed it,

> We have the means to end hunger on the planet and to feed the world's six billion people. For the well-fed to spearhead campaigns and suppress research into potential solutions for ideological or pseudo-scientific reasons is downright irresponsible and immoral.[43]

Those who really depend upon traditional farming, whether in the past or in poorer countries today, in other words, are unlikely to hold such views. This conveniently ignores the well-documented strength of opposition to GM among those same traditional farmers and poorer countries,[44] which the biotech companies have decided, on their own initiative, to help.

Conclusion

The upshot of this chapter is that evaluative arguments are not advanced as strongly as they might be by those opposed to GM. Part of the problem has been that they have accepted the pro-GM terms of engagement. The battle is being fought on entirely quantitative and utilitarian grounds. Retreating in the face of ridicule, organised opposition has allowed other kinds of argument to be marginalised, almost as though embarrassed to be associated with them. Yet in addition to the measurable threat to biodiversity and health, there are many other reasons to oppose GM. No substantial answer has been advanced to the views that it represents an unwelcome discontinuity with positive values of the past; that it shows no humility or wonder at the goodness which comes from Nature (albeit sometimes aided or redirected by humans through cultivation) and no trust in the overall power of Nature (notwithstanding its concurrent destructiveness) to sustain and regenerate both itself and ourselves; that it undervalues the personal and cultural importance of Nature as a force for good in art, religion, literature and recreation.

There are many reasons not to agree with the recurrent arguments that genetic engineering is the same kind of intervention as traditional breeding. Traditional breeding works together with Nature, slowly and sensitively, by serendipity and observation, harnessing rather than overturning natural forces. Genetic engineering, on the other hand, works against it, rushing change without consideration or reflection, in a way that is at odds with evolutionary time,[45] overturning rather than respecting what it finds. As often observed by the pro-GM lobby, it is true that conventional intensive farming had already disrupted this harmony even before the advent of GM. Intensive farming has already decimated many of the materially useless – but psychologically uplifting – species of wild flowers, birds and butterflies on farmland. Yet GM has seemed to many the culmination and apogee of a destructive and dangerous process which dissociates us from an agriculture operating in concert with Nature rather than against it, one in which agricultural land is shared with other species rather than taken from them.

7

METAPHORS AND COMPARISONS

The rhetorical strategies in the GM debate make it part of a larger complex of issues. Through metaphors and comparisons, GM has become entangled with themes of warfare, terrorism, intercultural conflict and religious difference. In the intricate web of cross-references which emerges, the boundaries between what is merely figurative and what is literal are not always clear.

Conceptual clusters

Debates over science and technology have a tendency to draw upon the issues of their time. It is revealing to compare the GM controversy with earlier ones, such as that launched in 1962 by Rachel Carson's book *Silent Spring* about the use of chemicals in farming and their impact upon wildlife, whose title presages a world without birdsong in the spring. This book was a phenomenal success in its own time, and has been widely acknowledged since as one which fundamentally changed perceptions of the environment.[1] Analysing the powerful auditory image of its title, Brigitte Nerlich[2] argues that, although it does refer to a literal truth (chemicals in farming *do* reduce bird populations and thus birdsong), it also linked with other developments of the time, such as 'the atomic bomb, the cold war, the space race', and in particular fears of the aftermath of nuclear war. From all the effects of chemicals on farming, Carson singled out, very effectively, one with potent symbolic and cultural power: birdsong. The important point is not whether the prediction of a silent spring is factually accurate (sadly, it probably is) but that this particular choice galvanised opposition by drawing upon both ancient imagery and current political concerns. Such conceptual clusterings are far from uncommon.

If we move forward from the 1960s to the 1980s we find that descriptions of AIDS, rather than treating it as a matter for medical science, were conceived in terms linking it with other preoccupations of the period about political subversion and infiltration, and racial and sexual difference.[3] GM food, as we shall see, behaves in the same way, and draws to itself the preoccupations of the late 1990s and early 2000s. If it had appeared at a different point in history it might have been conceived on both sides in very different terms.

The physical nature of a new phenomenon, in other words, does not constitute the entirety of its role in contemporaneous discourse. It is appropriated and amplified, but also further understood, as a metaphor. It then both draws upon, and contributes to, understanding of other arenas. The phrase 'genetic engineering' is itself a metaphor equating the development of new crops with the construction of machines and buildings, thus making it seem to be part of a different field of human enterprise. Its successor 'genetic modification' evokes perhaps, though rather more vaguely, images of craftsmanship and repair, creating an image of work on a smaller scale more suited to a 'post-industrial' computer age. These original associations, however, have somewhat faded through frequent use, making both 'dead metaphors' (ones which we no longer consciously register) and freeing them up to be used in new ways. Prominent images in the current discourse of GM are of invasion and terror, contamination and impurity. They resonate with allusion to cultural and religious differences, and to deep divisions of belief about the relation between humanity and other species.

Battle, invasion and attack

We have encountered metaphors of warfare and invasion several times already. President Bush referred to a 'battle against disease' and Tony Blair saw Europe as 'overrun by protestors and pressure groups'. Lord May linked proponents of organic farming with Hitler and the Taliban, and in a later newspaper article[4] went on to describe campaigners on both sides as 'GM warriors'. Such metaphors of battle are frequent in the discourse of both opponents and proponents. Thus anti-GM campaigner George Monbiot writes of 'the covert biotech war' and how 'the battle to put a corporate GM padlock on our foodchain is being fought on the net' (*Guardian*, 19 November 2002). Michael Meacher is quoted as saying 'the GM food lobby had already won its battle in America' (*The Times*, 20 June 2003). Headlines refer to the 'BATTLE OF THE FOOD CHAIN' (*Guardian*, 17 May 2003) and 'BLAIR LOSES GM BATTLE' (*Daily Mail*, 3 July 2003) while in newspapers on both sides the dispute between the USA and EU is frequently described in terms such as:

> The battle over GM crops . . . GM foods in first assault of EU trade battle. . . . The US led 12 countries into a battle in the World Trade Organisation. . . . America is determined to win a wider trade battle over agriculture.
>
> (*The Times*, 14 May 2003)

> this epic battle for food dominance
>
> (*Guardian*, 17 May 2003)

The word 'attack' is curiously ambivalent. Sometimes it refers to verbal attacks made by one side or the other, elsewhere to physical attacks on crops, either by pests and weeds or by demonstrators taking direct action. 'Invaders' too may be either people or plants. GM crops are described by the opposition as giving rise to 'invasive superweeds' (*Guardian*, 29 November 2002); the pro-GM side describes them – using the emotive and nationalist 'our' – as 'unlikely to invade our countryside' (*The Times*, 22 July 2003). Protests are also frequently described as 'invasions': 'the invasion of the field by anti-GM demonstrators',[5] 'Greenpeace's invasion' (*Guardian*, 4 June 2003), etc.

Just as the image of the silent spring caught the imagination of the Cold War era, obsessed as it was with the possibility of nuclear war, so the themes of invasion resonate in a period of mass migration and ethnic and religious conflict, whether perceived as localised (Bosnia, Palestine, Rwanda, the Punjab, Kashmir, Chechnya . . .) or global, in the tension between Islam and the West.

Terrorism and Iraq

Metaphors of warfare may relate to particular wars. Three which dominated the beginning of the new millennium were the 'war against terrorism' declared by President Bush after 9/11, and the two more conventional ones which followed, first against Afghanistan in October 2001, then against Iraq in March 2003. In the news of this period, it is significant that the word 'attack' commonly collocates with 'terrorist', and 'invasion' with 'of Iraq' – another comparison to which we now turn in more detail.

Both for opponents and proponents, issues relating to these wars and the GM debate often seem to be part and parcel of the same thing. An obvious reason is that both campaigns – for GM food and against Iraq and terrorism – were launched in the USA, both were the occasion for bitter disagreements with Europe, and both gave rise to concern about US policy and motives. Opponents of US policy in the Gulf saw the campaign as an attempt to control oil supplies; opponents of GM food saw its development as an attempt to control the world's food supply. The report on the government-funded 'GM nation?' debate in Britain notes that:

> Comments on the debate were often coloured by suspicion over the motives for holding it. People attacked the debate as 'window-dressing', cover for a decision already made. This was often compared to the government's attitudes to protests against the Iraq war.[6]

And in the press of the time we find frequent parallels drawn:

> GM food: This is much worse than the intercontinental split over Iraq, if measured by the distance between the two views. At least, in the case of Saddam Hussein, both Europe and the US agreed that he was a bad guy. There is no similar accord on GM.
>
> (*The Times*, 25 June 2003)

> Michael Meacher . . . said Mr Blair should not ignore the report. 'We don't want GM to be Iraq Mark 2, where the evidence is very slight or even negative, where the great majority is opposed as over Iraq . . . and yet the Government goes ahead in the face of all the evidence,' he said.
>
> (*The Times*, 12 July 2003)

> Washington has backed away from threats to bring the European Union before the World Trade Organisation over the EU's refusal to allow the sale of genetically-modified produce. The US's official for agricultural affairs in London, Peter Kurz . . . denied that dropping the plans had anything to do with a desire to smooth relations with Europe before any conflict in Iraq.
>
> (*Guardian*, 21 February 2003)

In our own interviews and focus groups, conducted in 2001–3, similar connections were frequently made, particularly with the war in Iraq.

As for terrorism, we have already encountered this link several times: Lord May's equation of advocates of organic farming with 'fundamentalists' and the Taliban (p. 32), a scientist's description of protestors as 'terrorists' (p. 42), the anti-GM description of GM companies as 'bio-terrorists' (p. 54) and pro-GM claims – using the same word in a different sense – that GM plants could be used to detect 'bio-terrorist' attack (p. 50).

But it is hard to distinguish, in such a climate of accusation and association, the literal from the figurative. The very phrase 'war on terrorism' itself seems a mixture of the two. In the case of GM, it is unclear whether people are accused of actually *being* terrorists, or of having certain terrorist-*like* characteristics. To a degree, direct action against GM can be interpreted literally as sharing certain characteristics with terrorism. From the pro-GM standpoint, anti-GM activists *do* literally invade GM crop sites and – like terrorists – take direct physical action outside the law to achieve their ends. Extended, however, the analogy becomes insidious, for although there is indeed one point of comparison between the actions of terrorists and GM activists – direct action outside the law – damage to crops, even if regarded as illegal and wrong, can hardly be equated ethically with killing people.

Contamination, pollution, impurity

As with other frequently invoked terms, it is difficult to decide to what degree notions of 'contamination', 'pollution' and the 'impurity' which results from them are literal or metaphorical. Here it is important to distinguish between denotation and connotation. For while these terms can be taken prosaically (contamination/pollution = the presence of impurities; impurities = small quantities of another substance which change the nature of the original), it is hard to deny their overwhelmingly negative connotations. These are invoked by both sides. For the pro-GM lobby, genetic modification is a way of achieving purity, uncontaminated by weeds or pests; for the anti-GM lobby it is the genetically *un*modified which is pure, and the introduction of new genetic material which is the impurity.

Contamination results from 'colonisation', 'escape' and 'invasion', and thus appears to draw for both sides upon the discourses of race and migration. The Nuffield Council on Bioethics sophistically turns this notion on its head, associating opponents of GM with racism and, rather extraordinarily, 'tribes that kill twins at birth'.

Some critics of GM crops talk of cross-pollination from GM crops as 'pollution'. The concept of pollution has been said by some anthropologists to refer to illicit boundary-crossings, and they have thought that all cultures seem to have some conception of pollution because all cultures have some conception of 'things in the wrong place'. Sometimes the undesirability of pollution has a simple practical explanation. Grit in the oil will wreck the engine. Coal dust in the air will give us black lung. Not all sorts of wrongness have an easy explanation of that kind. Racism is an extreme, though wide-spread, symptom of the desire for purity. Indeed, many of the yearnings for 'natural purity' have little or no justification. Tribes that kill twins at birth appear to do so out of a sense that human beings are rightly born singletons and that only animals have multiple births, but they seem to take these drastic measures without much thought about exactly what would go wrong if they did not do so. Is it possible that some of the fear of GM crops is of the same sort?[7]

But the fear of 'mixing', the desire to preserve 'purity', and accusations of intolerance incurred by those who appeal to them, can be interpreted in opposite ways. On the one hand, it is true that opponents regard genetic modification as itself an act of contamination, and subsequent 'escapes' of pollen and plants as guilty of creating impurity. On the other hand, the result of GM farming is to create 'monocultures', eliminating both wild species and traditional mixed cropping.[8] 'Monoculture' is indeed a word thick with resonances of discourses other than farming. For while having a technical agricultural sense, it also evokes associations with the word 'culture' in its human sense, inviting comparison between a monocultural agriculture and the monocultural social world which many fear will be a result of globalisation.

This echo may remind us that agricultural terminology is loaded with standard metaphorical comparisons relating plants to human mental and spiritual life, so that apparently neutral uses of terms (reaping, sowing, seeds, harvests) inevitably burst with a potential to take on much more than their literal meaning. This is all too clear from the titles of works on GM, which almost invariably make some pun upon their subject matter: *Seeds of Deception*,[9] 'Seeds of doubt',[10] *Seeds of Trouble*,[11] *A Grain of Truth*,[12] *Bitter Harvest*.[13]

The title of this book, *Genetically Modified Language*, may seem to make a similar play on words, connecting two fields in a rather tenuous way. But there is more to the comparison than meets the eye. Uses of language and uses of land yield interesting comparisons. The contrast between monocultures and mixed crops, between fields in which all rival species are eliminated and those in which they are encouraged to thrive, has a very pertinent parallel with uses of discourse.[14] Insistence that scientific discourse alone is appropriate to discussion of GM is an attempt to reduce the options available to those wishing to engage with the debate. We are to have no mixed crop of varying perspectives upon the problem. Arguments are to grow in neat rows like the plants they seek to impose.

Religion and GM

Mention of other types of argument, as well as the metaphorical reference to the general conflict between the Islamic and Western world, may bring us to a perspective which has been in the background but not yet directly addressed. This is the relation of religious views to GM.

It is common to encounter a loose assumption that a-priori objections to GM are religious. In our own interviews, we observed that scientists equated ethical and religious views. Yet they also failed to distinguish between religions, or to specify any particular one, but we might assume that in a Western context the default reference for 'religion' is Christianity. At least one scientist we interviewed bracketed religious objections to GM with fundamentalist Christian creationism and its rejection of evolutionary theory. Lord May did the same, as we have seen in Chapter 2. This supposition that anti-GM views stem from religious conviction is rather more complex than is claimed. Ironically, in some cases, the opposite may be closer to the truth.

What are these assumptions based upon? Although there are undoubtedly Christian opponents of GM who interpret their faith as lending support to their views, they would be hard pressed to find biblical authority for them. Neither Old nor New Testament says much about the relation of humanity to other species. There is the reiterated reference to Man having been created 'in God's own image', implying a superiority over other species. The most specific and often-quoted statement on the subject, however, occurs in Genesis – ironically the same book which, when literally interpreted, is the source of the very creationism so often opposed by scientists. It runs as follows:

And God blessed them, and God said unto them, Be fruitful,
and multiply, and replenish the earth, and subdue it: and have
dominion over the fish of the sea, and over the fowl of the
air, and over every living thing that moveth upon the earth.
And God said, Behold, I have given you every herb bearing
seed, which is upon the face of all the earth, and every tree, in
the which is the fruit of a tree yielding seed; to you it shall be
for meat.

(Genesis 1:28–9)

This text has often been cited as evidence of divine authority for
human 'dominion' over all other species, though implying concomi-
tant responsibilities. As the Nuffield Council on Bioethics comments:

From a Judaeo-Christian perspective, it is an important truth
that God created nature for His own purposes, not merely for
our use, and that these purposes are important, indeed that it is
mandatory for us to respect nature as part of that creation.
Biblical premises yield positive duties as well as restrictions
on what we may do with the world, however. We have been
impressed by the emphasis placed by our Consultation
respondents from the Church of Scotland, and the Office of
the Chief Rabbi, among several others, on the duty laid on
humanity to 'cultivate and reorder nature'. God's gift is a
grant of sweeping authority to use the raw materials of
nature wisely, i.e. the stewardship principle. Indeed, it
would represent ingratitude for God's bounty to neglect the
materials placed before us. The parable of the talents is at
home in both Jewish and Christian thinking, and God's
injunction to 'be fruitful and multiply' is a moral injunction.
So far is orthodox Judaism, for instance, from restricting
scientific inquiry that we were told during the consultation
that orthodox Judaism has no problem with GM crops;
being kosher is not a question of biochemistry.[15]

Those Christian churches which have pronounced on GM have
tended (despite dissenting voices) to agree with the Chief Rabbi.
Thus the Vatican, in statements previewing a report in preparation,
has lent its support to GM, using arguments such as the following:

Archbishop Martino, who until last year was the Vatican
representative at the UN, said that he had lived for 16 years

in the US 'and I ate everything that was offered to me, including genetically modified products. They had no effect on my health. This controversy is more political than scientific.'[16]

Not exactly sound science! On the Protestant side, the Church of Scotland came down firmly on the side of GM too, using theological arguments based on Genesis:

> Drawing from the metaphors in the opening chapters of Genesis, we are a part of creation, made of dust, the same 'stuff' as the earth, formed from the same chemical elements, and we share with animals and plants the gift of life, with a shared genetic inheritance. Yet we have an additional dimension, expressed by the notion of being 'in the image of God', distinguishing us from the rest of creation. If this suggests special attributes, it also implies a special responsibility, in which God's image is expressed as a priestly calling in the creative, imaginative and caring way we are to act in nature, on God's behalf. As the Dutch theologian Egbert Schroten has pointed out, there is here a proper sense in which we are called to 'play God'. . . . it is hard to argue that genetic engineering to help produce food falls in the negative sense of playing God – something inherently wrong, and therefore forbidden.[17]

Assumptions that Judaeo-Christian theology lends support to opposition to GM, in other words, seem to be unfounded. Indeed, far from being at odds with religious fundamentalism, the GM industry seems to share some of its premises. You may remember (see Chapter 4, p. 69) that one of the Monsanto web pages described the company as 'capable *stewards* of the technologies we develop' (my emphasis). This biblical word is an unusual choice, and seems to echo the theological concept of 'stewardship' derived from Genesis and referred to in the Nuffield report. It may be significant that the GM industry has its heartland in the 'Bible belt' of the deeply Christian USA[18] – a connection to which Monsanto itself has drawn attention by the punning description of this area as the 'Bio belt'.[19]

But what of other religions? In Islam, which has no central religious institutions, there are views on both sides, although a search of Muslim websites in English reveals a preponderance against GM, reflecting perhaps important theological differences from Christianity and Judaism on the topic. The notion of man being created in God's image is considered unacceptable in a majority of Muslim traditions, since God cannot be described or defined in comparison to humans. Although the Koran refers in several places to the creation of Adam 'out of dust', it does not recount the story in the same way as the Bible, and has no equivalent to the biblical verses about dominion. On the contrary, Muslim opponents of GM can even find verses which – though admittedly open to many interpretations – they see as having the opposite meaning reflecting a very different attitude towards Nature and perhaps yet another dimension of the Islamic–Western divide.

> Eat and drink of that which Allah has provided and do not act corruptly, making mischief on the earth.
>
> (Koran 2:60)

> Certainly the creation of the heavens and the Earth is greater than the creation of the men, but mostly people do not know.
>
> (Koran 40:57)

> All the creatures on earth, and all the birds that fly with wings, are communities like you. We did not leave anything out of this book. To their Lord, all these creatures will be summoned.
>
> (Koran 6:38)

On the other hand, there are elements of Islam which could be interpreted as resembling the concept of dominion, though with important and subtle differences. After the fall Adam is forgiven and becomes God's *khalifa* (translated as 'vice-regent') on Earth, a title which, though initially adopted by successive Islamic rulers,[20] also incurs a general responsibility. As one commentary describes it,

> According to the teachings of Islam, all human beings are commanded to fulfil their individual roles as viceregents of God. [They] have been given the necessary mental intelligence and physical strength to study nature and its order so that they may then use their faculties, in accordance with nature and the moral guidelines ordained by God, to benefit humanity.[21]

In addition, modern Islamists make much of the concept of *maslahah* (translated as 'public interest'), insisting that for Muslims scientific progress needs to be consonant with the needs of the community. Many modern innovations, previously regarded as objectionable by conservative religious leaders, have been admitted under this rubric. Yet whether GM technology is among these will depend, crucially, upon whether it is regarded as actually in the general interest or not.

Like Islam, both Hinduism and Buddhism seem to give rise to more opposition to GM than support, making Judaism and Christianity the exceptions rather than the rule among religious attitudes to GM. It is important to note, however, that it is the establishment voices in these two faiths, rather than their rank and file, who tend to regard the issue in this way. Those Christians and Jews who do consider their opposition to be religious may perhaps unwittingly be drawing more upon some other more general religious tradition, perhaps with its roots in paganism, than upon their more modern faith.

'Beneficial species'

Both Monsanto and Syngenta talk of a need to protect 'beneficial species'.[22] But what exactly does this 'beneficial' mean? There are at least two alternatives. One is purely practical. Many species are beneficial to humanity in material terms, providing food, medicine or textiles. For example, the possible loss of the bumble bee as result of GM cultivation would deprive us of its honey. But another kind of benefit is not material. Skylarks – a species predicted to disappear from Britain within twenty years of commercial GM planting[23] – provide humans with a different kind of benefit through the inspiring beauty of their song in flight. This ambiguity in the word 'beneficial' poses a problem for the arguments of the GM lobby, for if it does include benefits of the latter kind, then the argument is de facto not entirely a scientific one (as the value of the skylark's song is not measurable) and such notions as 'interfering with Nature' are valid.

And what of species which not only bring no benefits, either materially or aesthetically, but are on the contrary positively harmful or dangerous? What of wasps, mosquitoes, rats, piranhas, sharks, poisonous snakes and the ticks carrying encephalitis and Lyme Disease? What argument can there be for preserving them? Of course they may turn out to be the source of some nutrient or medicine as yet unknown; they may play some crucial role in preserving an ecological system (aka 'the balance of Nature'!); and some of them at least, such as serpents and rats, are powerful cultural symbols and metaphors. But they can hardly be described as 'beneficial' in either sense. On their behalf a third line of reasoning is needed: one based upon a belief that all species have a right to survive, quite independently of the benefits or disadvantages they may have for humanity. Such a view, however, seems at odds with the views of the GM industry.

There are, then, at least three distinct lines of reasoning for preserving biodiversity: that it is a material resource; that it has non-material benefits; that it has some inherent right to survive. In practice, their application is considerably more complicated than this summary implies. The three are not easily kept separate. There are numerous fuzzy edges, and pay-offs to be made between one and another. The first criterion does not exclude the other two, nor the second the third. Thus arguments for the preservation of the bumble bee can draw upon all three. An opposite complexity arises when these three criteria conflict. Few would mourn the disappearance of the fatal encephalitis-carrying tick, and an intrinsic right to survival is unlikely to be extended to lethal viruses. There are times when the material benefits derived from one species may be regarded as outweighing the non-material benefits or intrinsic rights of others. Where food is concerned there is little compunction about the culling of competitors, parasites and predators. In farming, it is judged right that food crops should survive at the cost of 'weeds' and 'pests'. Yet 'weeds' and 'pests' are hardly scientific terms. They are only such from a human viewpoint, and, even then, one person's 'weeds' may be another person's wild flowers, or – for the other species that share our cultivated fields with us – their vital food supply.

This brings us to the heart of the problem: how these three criteria apply to land under cultivation, and the extent of the trade-off between benefit to humanity and harm to other species. The very act of cultivation inevitably displaces some and advantages others. Open-country species may thrive when forest is cleared for cultivation, while forest species by definition decline. Human existence entails interference with Nature to some degree. The issue is how much interference, of what kind, and in what circumstances. Should humanity seek to share cultivated land with other species, or further intensify monocultural farming, with wild species existing only on non-agricultural land? The easy bandying about of hooray phrases like 'beneficial species' fails to tackle these distinctions.

A fundamental disagreement

It might seem from current pro-GM arguments that the principle of preserving biodiversity on agricultural land is shared by both camps, the disagreement being only over which route is best. The current biotech arguments for genetic engineering seem to be based on reasonable premises of balance and pay-off of the kind I have just outlined. Central to their present arguments is the claim that yields must be increased at a time of burgeoning overpopulation, but in a way which will as far as possible preserve other species. Not so long ago, however, before the public outcry against GM, rather different ideas were prominent which are now kept discreetly out of sight. Just how deep this disagreement may be can be understood with reference to a doctrine referred to by the leading anti-GM writer Jeremy Rifkin as 'algenism'.[24] To explain it, he cites the following extract from a paper given at a symposium organised by Monsanto in 1985:

> As a consequence of recent advances in genetic engineering, [a biological species] must be viewed . . . as a depository of genes that are potentially transferable. A species is not merely a hard-bound volume of the library of nature. It is also a loose-leaf book, whose individual pages, the genes, might be available for selective transfer and modification of other species.[25]

That this is not a scientific statement, but rather an evaluative and ideological one, is evident in the strange use of the modal verb 'must' and the adverb 'merely'. It does not follow from the scientific facts about genes that species *must* be viewed in this way. There is no scientific reason to derogate the notion of species inviolability with the word 'merely' or with a rather dubious analogy between DNA and a book.[26] As Rifkin comments:

> An algenist views the living world as in potentia. In this regard, the algenist doesn't think of an organism as a discrete entity but rather as a temporary set of relationships existing in a fluid context, on the way to becoming something else. For the algenist, species boundaries are just convenient labels for identifying a familiar biological condition or relationship, but are in no way regarded as impenetrable walls separating animals or plants.[27]

Algeny is an approach at odds with the idea of preserving balance between species, because it abandons the notion of species. It promotes 'interference with Nature' not as a necessary evil but as a matter of principle. It is clearly an ideological rather than a scientific stance.

Part III

THE SPOKEN TO

8

PUBLIC POLITICS

So far, we have focused almost exclusively upon two points of the communicative triangle: those speaking for GM, and their perspective on the subject matter. We have looked in detail at the arguments of some of GM's most powerful advocates – a President and a Prime Minister, eminent and rank-and-file scientists, news reporters and columnists, company chairmen and PR departments. We have seen a variety of genres: speeches and proclamations, reports, articles, interviews and web pages. Despite the apparent variety, all these sources have two things in common. First, they are all consciously directed, at least in part, at the 'general public'. Second, they include a lot of talking about talking. Newspapers are preoccupied with reporting and analysing what others have said. Both governments and biotech companies commit themselves to 'listening' and to 'dialogue', while scientists constantly reiterate a wish to improve their communication of what they are doing. An image of the public – the missing point of the triangle – is therefore always present in what is being said. They are portrayed, indeed positioned by GM proponents, either as passive recipients of expert knowledge and wise decisions or as active participants through dialogue in the decision-making process.

The public to whom these arguments are addressed, however, seem often not to recognise this image of themselves, and to perceive the issues rather differently. Their position is not the one in which the pro-GM lobby would seek to place them. It is not just that they are, when asked, often against GM. They are also often against the people who advocate it, and the ways in which they do so. Thus some of the commonest objections are neither scientific nor ethical, but political. They express dismay that decisions are being taken undemocratically by unelected commercial companies, by the governments of other nations or by experts. They regard the supposed dialogue as bogus, they do not trust the information they are given, and they claim that irreversible decisions have already been taken without consultation.

The concept of a 'public' with an 'opinion', however, though widely used, is problematic. It is too general to be meaningful. Members of the public differ widely on every possible parameter, having radically different levels of education and experience, age, philosophy, belief, background, etc. In such a heterogeneous category, any single 'member of the public' is by definition atypical. In practice, moreover, who is and is not included varies with context. The scientists we interviewed clearly regarded 'scientists' and 'public' as mutually exclusive. Yet these scientists are in certain contexts members of the public too – as are politicians, journalists and company shareholders. A further problem is the issue of different national publics. Although GM is an international issue, it would be foolish to talk of an international public when nations are so different from each other.[1]

Bearing these problems in mind, this conclusion attempts to give a flavour of the response to the flood of words directed at the public by advocates of GM. The sources are from Britain, and are of two kinds. One is the public debate in Britain during 2003; the other, focus groups conducted in the same year. Both are partial – in both senses of the word. They reflect particular kinds of people: those who attend public meetings in the first case, those who agree to participate in focus groups in the second. They provide nevertheless an insight into the missing half of the 'dialogue' which advocates claim is taking place.

Organised debate in Britain[2]

In Britain, 2003 saw a series of meetings and consultations[3] aimed at 'the general public' and apparently pursuing a variety of purposes. Some were intended to inform people about GM, others to persuade them of its benefits or dangers, others still to provide fora for concerns to be aired, sounding out opinions and attitudes along lines familiar in market research.

In the midst of this activity, an altogether different debate was being prepared, following a set of recommendations by the Agricultural and Environment Biotechnology Commission.[4] Its aim was to involve the public in decision-making about a possible future commercialisation of GM crops, and to allow them, to a certain extent, to 'frame' the issues and decide the format of the events themselves.[5] The idea was not only unprecedented, at least in Britain, but was intended to provide, if successful, a blueprint for policy-making about other technological innovations, possibly in other contentious areas.

Although the British government declared its support for this exercise[6] and provided a timetable and funding, it left organisational detail to a steering board. It seemed also, despite the usual hedging, to make some commitment to acting on the results, while reserving the right to weigh them against the results of two other parallel strands of investigation – a Scientific Review and a Costs and Benefit Review. Each of these held its own events (some of which were open to the public) and reported[7] to the government in the autumn of 2003.

The debate involved a mixture of national, regional and local events. Inevitably, their structure and organisation attracted criticisms from both sides. Funding was seen as too low, even after it was doubled from a quarter to half a million pounds. Publicity was meagre, and access to the events not always easy. The Central Office for Information, managing the everyday business, was said to be both inexperienced and unenthusiastic. There were charges of infiltration: that most participants were from organisations already committed to one side or the other. Yet the difficulties encountered in organising and running the process were perhaps commensurate with the novelty and scale of the endeavour, and at the end the Steering Board produced a report[8] which, despite any shortcomings in the process, was generally accepted by both sides as giving some insight into what the 'general public' thought about GM. In the executive summary, the 'key messages' were summarised under the following headings:

1 People are generally uneasy about GM.
2 The more people engage in GM issues, the harder their attitudes and more intense their concerns.
3 There is little support for early commercialisation.
4 There is widespread mistrust of governments and multinational companies.
5 There is broad desire to know more and for further research to be done.
6 Developing countries have special interests.
7 The debate was welcomed and valued.[9]

The process was, then, to some extent successful, and its findings clear. Yet the exercise should also be judged, it seems reasonable to say, by whether the end results, as well as the process, met the original objectives. Did the findings contribute to government policy-making, as they were supposed to do?

According to the official report, among participants, even before the debate was concluded, there was a

> strong and wide degree of suspicion about the motives, intentions and behaviour of those taking decisions about GM – especially government and multinational companies.
>   . . . a weakening of faith in the ability or even the will of any government to defend the interest of the general public.

There was also 'suspicion that the Government has already taken a decision about GM. Crucially, the public are found to be concerned that the debate has only been a camouflage and its results will be ignored.'[10]

Events seem to have borne out these views. The British government has never said whether or how it will incorporate the findings of the 'GM nation' debate into any policy.

Focus groups

Our own focus group research,[11] conducted in the same year, replicated these findings about public mistrust in the bigger debate. We ran six focus groups, selected to reflect the views of groups of people with particular reasons for interest in the issue. They were:

- birdwatchers, for their knowledge of wildlife
- farmers,[12] for their knowledge of changes to agriculture and their impact
- temporary residents from poor countries, for their views on arguments that GM agriculture would feed the world
- young adults, for their concerns for the future
- parents of young children, for their particular concerns about diet, health and their children's future
- voluntary charity workers, for their social responsibility and commitment.

Each group was shown short extracts from texts about GM, including the speeches by Tony Blair and Lord May analysed in Chapter 1, and short extracts from newspapers. They were asked to give their reaction, both to what was said and to the language. As in the national debate, mistrust of politicians and commercial companies was a dominant theme. Here are sixteen extracts giving a sample of their reactions.[13] It is inevitably a partial selection (again in both senses of the word) but it does represent very well the overwhelming drift of the views we encountered. (An asterisk indicates a change of speaker.)

1.

* I think the same thing would happen as what's happened to all these others I've ever been involved in. It'll end up in a pigeon hole gathering dust, and democracy's seen to work, and we'll do what we're told at the end of the day.

2.

* I don't know I just do not know what how we could have an organised national debate on something like this. But there must be a way. It could be the case that if you went through any kind of process you would find afterwards that decision had already been made before it ever started. So I don't know.

3.

* The government has decided what it wants to do and it's going to do it, and really what we do isn't really going to make an awful lot of difference you know.
* They're not going to take any notice of what we say.
* No.
* If it's not in accordance with what the government were thinking in the first place.

4.

* Well 18 per cent of the world's farmland is now producing GM food. That's nearly a fifth already . . . And we're only debating it now.

5.

* I don't think it's going to make any difference anyway . . . it's here.

6.

* I think personally individually we probably all feel insignificant in that area. I'm speaking for myself because I feel I always am preaching an uphill battle anyway. . . . It's like voting for a party isn't it? The majority of people you speak to, they [say] does it really matter at the end of the day whoever gets in? They're going to tell you a pack of lies anyway, and they're only going to be in it for their own purposes. That's the way I think.

7.
* I don't see how you can get your opinion through to be honest or to be taken note of.

8.
* Well I don't think people's opinions are being heard these days.

9.
*I just feel it's all being driven by big business.
* Yes it is.
* I think people are getting backhanders to push this through.
* That's it. That's it. You're right.
* I think that's what's happened.
* Yes.
. . .
* I agree with what she said. It's just big business. It's the big corporates and the American companies and probably some in Europe that have a big say. And of course they must be giving these politicians backhanders, because they're pushing these things through unbeknown to the rest of the public, which is not right. . . . We're going to be told by Brussels how many GM crops we can plant in our country and we have no say in it, and that can't be right.
. . .
* We don't have a say in a lot of things do we?
* No, no.
* You know, it's happened before we find out about it.
* That's right.
* It's already happened.
* That's right.

10.
* No matter what I said the government make their own mind up anyway.
* I think what you'd have to [do is] vote us all into Cabinet wouldn't you?
* There's such a big majority, the Labour government, I don't think the government particularly listen to what the vast majority of people in Britain want.

11.
* We can only make a petition to the MP.

* . . . and that's as far as you'll get isn't it? Nothing will happen.

12.
* If you don't get emotional about something nothing seems to change. So I think that if people's reaction is being demonstrated in an emotional way it might be considered un-British, but I think Britain has now seen that the only way that you can get something changed is by making some form of demonstration.
* Yes.
* So it's very easy for someone to say we can get emotional about this. I get emotional about a lot of things, and I thank God for that. Because you know we have a feeling that can be expressed, and if we haven't then we haven't got a democracy.

13.
* That's why there's a debate. To my mind the problem with GM is nobody knows anything about it . . .
* Well scientists don't know, do they, the answer the long term answer.
* They won't have anything to do with what they developed. They'll only let you know what they want you to know.
* Well yes but . . .
* No matter what they develop. I mean who cares, or whatever, you know.
* It's a free country, as long as you do as you're told.

14.
* There is no democracy over the introduction of GM is there?
* No.
* No.
* But in a way there is no democracy in any case. We are as much slaves as the ancient Spartans were, but in a different way.
* Yes.
* I mean, OK, all right, another classical allusion. We are given bread and circuses to keep us quiet as long as we keep going. We are herded by the politicians in the direction that they want us to go, and if any of us are daft enough to want to either dig our heels in, or look over the hedge, or turn round and go back again, they're not going to have it.
* Yes we really live in what do you call an elected dictatorship don't we?

* Yes.
* We do yes.
* You know we're not a democracy as such are we?
* That's right.

15.

* I think the challenges really are to make certain it's done properly, that people are aware of what we're getting, that they're not trying to do anything underhand. Because we've got to the age we just don't trust the people that are trying to put this forward. Because they keep ducking and diving all the time. And then it disappears, and then it comes back again, and everybody has to start again. And thinking about it, I feel as if it's all being sneaked in by the back door.

16.

* But what I'm saying is that that cannot happen because you've got a third party involved in the situation which is the multi-nationals. The government are not sufficiently strong to resist the multinationals. We're seeing it happen in America. The government of America is not run by the politicians. It's run by the big companies. . . . I'm talking about the relationship between the government. They are not free agents to set up an even-handed situation like you would envisage.

Such views present a curious communicative phenomenon. Members of the public have been exposed to a rhetorical whirlwind, battering them from all sides. They are told that GM is good for them by a host of authoritative sources: the White House, the Vatican, Downing Street, other political and religious leaders, learned societies, university scientists, government commissions, international corporations, commercial leaders and some of the press. This onslaught has deployed every persuasive rhetorical strategy imaginable: from august oratory to the chattiest synthesised egalitarianism, from broadsheet bombast to tabloid humour, from complex philosophy to advertising and PR. It has compared GM with the greatest of human achievements, and its opponents to Nazis and terrorists. One might expect the combination of such power and persuasiveness to have succeeded. The participants in our focus groups were much less eloquent than those trying to persuade them – as is readily apparent from the quotations above. They were also, as they frankly admit, much less knowledgeable about the technicalities of GM. There was surely every reason for them, having listened to the arguments, to adjust their views: to think differently of those speaking to them, of what was being spoken about, and of their own role and rights in the debate – until their communicative triangle fitted neatly and obediently onto the one presented to them.

A long-established metaphor can provide an interesting way of expressing this. It is common to compare our reception of language to food. We talk of a diet of ideas, of digesting what we read, of swallowing an unpleasant truth and so on. We might consider it to be – like the comparisons of warfare and argument, or seeds and ideas discussed in Chapter 7 – to be a fundamental metaphor structuring the way we think about language.[14] To extend the comparison, where arguments for GM are concerned it seems that an attempt at force-feeding has resulted in the opposite effect from that intended. People have been fed but have not swallowed. Or to use the eating metaphor in a different way, they are fed up.

For all their power, the arguments for GM have not succeeded. To a degree, there is nothing new in this phenomenon. Human beings are naturally sceptical. Propaganda campaigns have often been seen through. Yet there may also be something new happening, both in language use and in reactions to it. In the past, propaganda made no pretence of treating the recipients as equal participants. Now there is a constant pretence that we are taking decisions 'together'.

There is an analogy here between what is being done to crops and what is being done to words. One view of GM technology is that it is just an extension of past practices. As the Speaker of the House in the USA expressed it, 'since the dawn of time, farmers have been modifying plants to improve yields and create new varieties resistant to pests and diseases. . . . Biotechnology is merely the next stage of development in the age-old process.[15]

In a similar way, one might say that 'since the dawn of time', authorities and experts have been trying to persuade a gullible public to do what they are told. This too is an 'age-old process'. An alternative view is that something new is happening both to language use and to agriculture. The fake dialogue of the campaign for GM, and the assumption that its recipients will be persuaded, unsuccessfully attempt to deny what is happening. Language, like Nature, is being used in an unnatural and unsuccessful way. A cause for optimism is that those without vested interests in GM technology remain critical of both GM and the language used to promote it. It is the truth of this comparison which justifies the title of this book: genetically modified language.

APPENDIX 1
DISPUTED FACTS

The purpose of this appendix is to give, for those readers who are unfamiliar with them, a brief overview of the main points of contention about the physical effects of GM agriculture.

A GM plant has been changed to have a characteristic which it did not have before. It may grow faster, flower or bear fruit at a different time of year, contain more nutrients, survive droughts and salinity, change colour or taste, kill the 'pests' which feed on it, remove chemicals from the soil, or be resistant to a particular chemical insecticide or herbicide. Changes of this kind inevitably raise the possibility that a GM crop will affect the people who eat it, the other living things around it, and the food which is produced from it.

The scientific debate about material consequences thus falls under two headings: human health and environmental impact. These two areas are often kept neatly fenced off from each other – although inevitably they interact. As the main concern of this book is with the language of the GM debate, this appendix is necessarily a brief résumé of these two areas, aimed only at giving enough background to examine the ways in which they are deployed in argument. Readers interested in further details can refer to the growing and extensive literature on both of these areas, though with the caution that research is moving and changing so fast that scientific opinion (as befits its provisional nature) is far from stable, that what was written only two or three years earlier has often been superseded. The arguments over GM agriculture, moreover, have coincided with a period of rapid revision in genetics in general. The finding of the human genome project that humans have far fewer genes than was expected,[1] has further upset the equation of single genes with characteristics (which is the basis of genetic engineering) and shifted attention even more strongly towards their expression and interaction.

Health

GM proponents frequently assert that there is as yet no definite relation between eating GM food and any particular health problem. For them, GM food is 'innocent until proved guilty'. Cause for concern is small, they claim, and should in any case be balanced against benefits. Some GM opponents take a very different view. Some believe there is already evidence of adverse health effects.[2] Even those who accept that there is as yet no decisive evidence of harm are still quick to point out that there are serious reasons for concern. For them, the key phrase is 'as yet'. They emphasise the provisional nature of the theory that GM food is not harmful, accuse government and industry of avoiding or distorting research on key questions, and demand further investigation before it can be declared safe for humans.

Let us deal first with this opposition view. First, they argue, given that GM food has only been produced commercially since 1996, it is simply too early to judge. Second, they say, there has been research indicating dangers.[3] The cause célèbre was an experiment by Dr Arpad Pusztai at the Rowett Research Institute. In 1995 Pusztai and his colleagues began modifying potatoes by adding to them a special type of lectin made by snowdrops to deter sap-sucking insects. These GM potatoes were then fed to rats. His conclusion was that, in contrast to other lectin-rich potatoes, the GM potatoes were causing changes with health consequences to the rats' internal organs. In 1999, his findings were published in the *Lancet*, the leading British medical journal. More controversially, when interviewed on the British TV programme *World in Action*, he warned of possible consequences to human health, saying that, in his view, consumers were effectively being used as guinea pigs. Here we have a slippage from a claim which, even if wrong, is scientific in nature (GM potatoes damage rats' internal organs) to one which, even if right, is a non-scientific one (the public are being used as guinea pigs).

Pusztai's claims of possible health risks, despite the fact that they had been peer-reviewed six times before publication, were hotly disputed on scientific grounds, and described, for example, by the Royal Society as 'flawed'.[4] But they were not the only claims of dangers to health. In 2002, the Royal Society itself concluded[5] that GM technology might 'lead to unpredicted harmful changes in the nutritional nature of food', possibly causing a plant 'to become allergenic'. It recommended further research into the inclusion of GM food in the diets of young children and pregnant or breast-feeding women. Also in 2002, research commissioned by the Food Standards Agency,[6] concluded[7] that GM crop material was finding its way into human gut bacteria: a finding which in turn raised the fear that the marker genes[8] might lead to resistance to antibiotics in humans.

All these suggestions of health hazards have been seized upon by the opposition to GM. One particularly eloquent opponent has been Michael Meacher, British Environment Minister from 1997 to 2003. Following his dismissal from government, and writing with the benefit of inside knowledge, he made a scathing attack on the British government's GM policy.[9] Summarising the reasons for caution over the health consequences of GM food, he points not only to the research which *has* been done but also to areas in which, suspiciously, much-needed research *has not* been done. For example, he counters the frequent pro-GM assertion that millions of North Americans have been consuming GM food without adverse consequences by pointing to the absence of any supporting scientific evidence to this claim. He suggests that the doubling of food-derived illnesses in the US since the introduction of GM food, and the 50 per cent increase in soya allergies in the UK following the importing of GM soya, while not necessarily linked to the consumption of GM ingredients, should be matters for urgent scientific investigation.

GM proponents, however, not only reject such claims, or say that they have been distorted; they have also turned the issue on its head, claiming that not only is GM food not dangerous to health, it can even be advantageous. Crops can be modified to provide very specific health benefits. The flagship example is 'golden rice': a case cited regularly and religiously as a GM solution to a major world health problem, Vitamin A deficiency (VAD). This is a condition common in countries where rice is the staple diet; its effects are particularly severe for children. According to the World Health Organisation in 2001,[10] it contributes to over a million child deaths a year, as well as widespread blindness. One of the causes of the condition is the removal of the leaves and husks (containing beta-carotene which converts to Vitamin A in the body) when the rice is milled and polished to improve storage. In GM golden rice, however, the introduction of a gene from daffodils ensures that beta-carotene is produced in the dehusked grain. It also endows the plant's endosperm with the colour from which the modified crop takes its name – although the connotations of 'golden' are much wider than mere colour, and the use of this word has as much to do, one suspects, with marketing as with objective description.

But the argument for health benefits does not stop with 'golden rice'. Soya may shortly be modified to contain more ferritin which reduces iron deficiency. Tomatoes may contain lycopene which is thought to protect against prostate cancer, or flavanoid which may reduce cardiovascular disease. Extra Vitamin C may reduce cholesterol. Tobacco may be grown without nicotine.[11] A GM potato known as the 'protato' might be developed to contain at least a third more protein than normal tubers and so enhance the diets of malnourished children.[12] More generally, in the 'new generation', already under way, there is 'pharming' of 'nutraceuticals', by which plants are modified to produce medicines and drugs. There is really no end to the potential modifications of this kind – and no end to the arguments which can be advanced both for and against each one of them.

The scientific fact that plants can be modified to deliver such effects sounds like a winning argument which only the most callous anti-GM fanatic could dismiss. Yet, as always in the GM debate, there is a counter-argument, with its own evidence. On the subject of golden rice, for example, opponents point out that the crop – which is in any case still 'only a research product that needs considerable further development before it will be available to farmers and consumers'[13] – is not an efficient source of Vitamin A, as the beta-carotene may not be in a form which is easily absorbed and because, in the absence of any other source of Vitamin A, a person would need to eat 9 kilos a day to satisfy required intake. They argue that there are many ways of combating VAD which are both cheaper and more efficient. Dietary supplements could take people out of Vitamin A deficit. Rice storage techniques could be improved to allow retention of natural beta-carotene. What VAD sufferers most need, they continue, are 'natural' sources of Vitamin A such as eggs, milk, butter, fish, green vegetables and fruit.[14] Indeed, they point out, there was once, ironically, such a source readily available in the rice-eating communities where VAD is now so rampant: the vegetable Bathua, the traditional source of Vitamin A, which has now been eliminated as a weed from the rice fields by herbicides.[15] In other words, the biotech companies, their opponents claim, are 'solving' a problem of their own creation.

GM crops and biodiversity

The second strand in the scientific debate concerns the effects which GM crops might have on the wildlife around them. There are two issues of contention.

The first issue concerns the danger of GM crops spreading either by cross-pollination with non-GM crops or by establishing themselves outside the area where they were planted. On this there has been a good deal of disagreement about the evidence. Opponents cite cases for escaped or contaminated populations.[16] Proponents have claimed either that such cases are rare or that GM strains are 'typically wimps' that cannot compete in the wild, in contrast to the 'real problems' of introduced non-GM 'invasive species'.[17]

This issue of scientific research into cross-fertilisation bears uncanny similarities to those surrounding research into GM health effects, and the controversy over the research by Arpad Pusztai. After studying native varieties of Mexican maize, David Quist and Ignacio Chapela reported evidence that transgenic DNA from GM varieties had contaminated native strains of Mexican maize and become unstable within it. The results of the research were published in *Nature* after being peer-reviewed by three referees.[18] Like Pusztai, Chapela found his research challenged immediately as seriously flawed – most strongly by colleagues in his own faculty at the University of California at Berkeley. He also reported being threatened by a senior Mexican government official, and being asked by him to retract his findings and come up with others more favourable to pro-GM policies.[19] A BBC radio documentary suggested that the opposition within his own faculty was not unconnected to its receipt, some years earlier, of a $25 million grant from the biotech company Novartis (now part of Syngenta), and that the Mexican government's antagonism to him was in response to pressure from the US embassy.[20] Chapela's research has not been alone, however. In 2003, British government research showed that GM oilseed rape readily cross-pollinates with other non-GM varieties.[21]

The second environmental issue concerns the effects of GM crops with resistance to a specific herbicide or insecticide. Plants modified in this way can be treated differently from conventional ones. For example, rather than being treated with an array of different herbicides, 'herbicide-tolerant' plants can be subjected to one 'broad-spectrum herbicide' removing all of the 'weeds' around it – everything, in other words, except the plant itself. It is in considering the effects of this on biodiversity that the proponents and the opponents disagree so bitterly. Proponents argue that this single-dose strategy will actually reduce the amount of chemicals used, replacing the usual frequent sprayings with fewer doses, thus leaving less chemical residue to enter the food chain and allowing insect and plant life to recover after the initial spraying. Opponents claim that some of the particular chemicals used can have disastrous effects on everything else that lives around the plant – from the micro-organisms in the soil, through insects, right up to birds and the animals at the top end of the food chain.

As with health and gene transfer, the history of the scientific research into direct damage to biodiversity follows a familiar pattern. Yet, considering the possible scale of such damage, it is remarkable that in those countries where GM crops are grown legally, approval has not been more dependent upon prior research into such issues. One famous, though contested, finding concerns the monarch butterfly whose population, according to research published in 1999, suffered from stopovers in fields of GM corn on its spectacular migratory journey from Canada to Mexico.[22] It was not until October 2003 that the results of the British government Farm Scale Evaluations severely upset pro-GM claims by clearly showing the detrimental effects of GM oilseed rape and fodder beet on both insects and wild plant seeds.[23] By removing their staple food, both of these effects would have very severe consequences for bird life.[24] Yet even these, though 'the largest and most thorough of their kind in the world',[25] were severely limited in scope, examining direct effects only on seeds and invertebrates, only in the short term, and only in a British environment.

A further environmental issue is raised by the biotech claim that crops can be modified to grow on so-called 'marginal' land, including, for example, salt flats.[26] Although GM proponents claim that this will help poorer farmers by making available more arable land and will simultaneously protect the environment by making them 'less inclined to carve out new land from rain forests because their old fields were exhausted',[27] both claims can be contested. Very little research has in fact been done on modification for such purposes, and in any case what is marginal land agriculturally is also often home to endangered species.

GM proponents have three strategy options on environmental issues. They can contest existing evidence of gene flow or chemical damage, claiming that neither is significant. This option is hard, as they must prove a negative. Alternatively, and more persuasively, they can acknowledge that GM crops do cause some damage to biodiversity, but invoke a 'lesser of two evils' argument by claiming that the damage is less with GM crops than with conventional intensive farming. This tactic was undermined by the FSE results showing the negative impact of two of the three crops studied. Even the claim that (in Britain at least[28]) the third crop, GM maize, might cause less damage to biodiversity than conventional maize was skewed by the fact that the conventional crop in the comparison had been sprayed with Atrazine, a chemical already being phased out owing to the environmental damage which it causes. Alternatively, proponents can approach the issues more indirectly, pointing to supposed increased yields, and claiming that, although there may be damage to biodiversity in areas under GM cultivation, given an ever-increasing world population, further intensification of agriculture is the only way to avoid further extension of cultivation while producing constant supplies of food, 'continuing', as the Syngenta website puts it, 'to increase yields without using more land or bringing wild habitats into cultivation'.[29]

APPENDIX 2
'MY 10 FEARS FOR GM FOOD'
(CONCLUDED)

The rest of the article by HRH The Prince of Wales in the *Daily Mail*, Tuesday, 1 June 1999, the first four points of which appear on pp. 19–21 (reproduced for copyright reasons), reads as follows:

5. Is it sensible to plant test crops without strict regulations in place?

Such plants are being planted in this country now – under a voluntary code of practice. But English Nature, the Government's official adviser on nature conservation, has argued that we ought to put strict, enforceable regulations in place first.

Even then, will it really be possible to prevent contamination of nearby wildlife and crops, whether organic or not? Since bees and the wind don't obey any sort of rules – voluntary or statutory – we shall soon have an unprecedented and unethical situation in which one farmer's crops will contaminate another's against his will.

6. How will consumers be able to exercise genuine choice?

Labelling schemes clearly have a role to play. But if conventional and organic crops can become contaminated by GM crops grown nearby, those people who wish to be sure they are eating or growing absolutely natural, non-industrialised, real food, will be denied that choice. This seems to me wrong.

7. If something goes wrong with a GM crop, who will be held responsible?

It is important that we know precisely who is going to be legally liable to pay for any damage – whether it be to human health, the environment or both. Will it be the company who sells the seed or the farmer who grows it? Or will it, as was the case with BSE, be all of us?

8. Are GM crops really the only way to feed the world's growing population?

This argument sounds suspiciously like emotional blackmail to me. Is there any serious academic research to substantiate such a sweeping statement?

The countries which might be expected to benefit certainly take a different view. Representatives of 20 African states, including Ethiopia, have published a statement denying that gene technologies will 'help farmers to produce the food that is needed in the 21st century'.

On the contrary, they 'think it will destroy the diversity, the local knowledge and the sustainable agricultural systems . . . and undermine our capacity to feed ourselves'. How much more could we achieve if all the research funds currently devoted to fashionable GM techniques – which run into billions of dollars a year – were applied to improving methods of agriculture which have stood the test of time? We already know that yields from many traditional farming systems can be doubled, at least, by making better use of natural resources.

9. What effect will GM crops have on the people of the world's poorest countries?

Christian Aid has just published a devastating report, entitled *Selling Suicide*, explaining why GM crops are unlikely to provide solutions to the problems of famine and poverty. Where people are starving, lack of food is rarely the underlying cause.

It is more likely to be lack of money to buy food, distribution problems and political difficulties.

The need is to create sustainable livelihoods for everyone. Will GM crops really do anything to help? Or will they make problems worse, leading to increasingly industrialised forms of agriculture, with larger farms, crops grown for export while indigenous populations starve, and more displaced farm workers heading for a miserable degrading existence in yet more shanty towns?

10. What sort of world do we want to live in?

This is the biggest question of all. I raise it because the capacity of GM technology to change our world has brought us to a crossroads of fundamental importance.

Are we going to allow the industrialisation of Life itself, redesigning the natural world for the sake of convenience and embarking on an Orwellian future? And, if we do, will there eventually be a price to pay?

Or should we be adopting a gentler, more considered approach, seeking always to work with the grain of Nature in making better, more sustainable use of what we have, for the long-term benefit of mankind as a whole?

The answer is important. It will affect far more than the food we eat; it will determine the sort of world that we, and our children, inhabit.

NOTES

Introduction

1 <http://www.monsanto.com/monsanto/layout/sci_tech/ag_biotech/default.asp> (accessed 4 March 2004).

2 This description follows one by a Monsanto scientist on the BBC radio programme *Seeds of Trouble* (BBC Radio 4, 19 January 2003) and in Bains (1993: 42). Similar descriptions can also be found in two anti-GM sources: Smith (2003: 57) and <http://www.foodsafetynetwork.ca/gmo/antresgm.pdf> (accessed 15 January 2004).

3 This 'biolistics' method, once described as a 'favoured route' (Bains 1993: 255), is now being replaced by use of the bacterium *Agrobacteria tumifaciens*.

4 See Widdowson (1975: 47–70, 91–9; 2004).

5 C. James, 'Preview, global status of commercialized transgenic crops: 2002', ISAAA Brief No. 27, Ithaca, NY, 2002.

6 Reuters, 9 September 2003.

1 Politicians

1 <http://www.whitehouse.gov/news/releases/2001/05/20010517–9.html> (accessed 6 June 2003).

2 In its most general sense 'biotechnology' means the 'use of micro-organisms to make an end product' or 'anything that improves human utilisation of animals and plants' and would thus include ancient processes such as wine fermentation and selective breeding (Hodson 1992: 72). But though the processes are old, the word is not. Hulse claims that it 'first appeared about 1905 in Leeds where a Bureau of Biotechnology provided chemical and microbiological consultant services to breweries in the North of England'. (Joseph H. Hulse, 'Agribusiness, biotechnologies and international trade – implications for bioscientists and bioengineers', seminar paper, University of Reading, 10 June 2002). Its use outside technical and scientific discourse, however, is much more recent. It was not

included at all, for example, in the 1940 edition of the *Shorter Oxford English Dictionary*.

3 In Malay the word *kita* means 'we-inclusive-of-addressee', while *kani* means 'we-exclusive-of-addressee'.

4 Bauer (2002) observes that while scientists may see the two as deriving from the same research, non-scientists tend to see them as quite separate, and apply different criteria to them.

5 <http://www.number-10.gov.uk/output/Page1715.asp> (accessed 6 June 2003).

6 Blair gave a speech on globalisation to the Confederation of Indian Industry in Bangalore on 5 January 2002.

7 Anybody with access to the Internet can try this out by visiting the 'sampler' site of the COBUILD corpus: <http://titania.cobuild.collins.co.uk/form.html>.

8 This concordance gives occurrences of 'overrun by' provided by the COBUILD sampler. More extensive analysis of the British National Corpus produces similar results.

9 Sinclair (1991); Louw (1993).

10 These were the three countries listed by President Bush in his State of the Union Address on 30 January 2002. He added Cuba, Libya and Syria in a later speech in May 2002.

11 For extended discussion of Blair's language, see Fairclough (2000).

12 For copyright reasons, the rest of this article is reproduced in Appendix 2.

13 Fishman (1980); Coates (1986: 105).

14 Tannen (1992: 227–9).

15 Bakhtin (1981: 304) describes a hybrid construction as 'an utterance that belongs, by its grammatical (syntactic) and compositional markers, to a single speaker, but that actually contains mixed within it two utterances, two speech manners, two styles, two "languages," two semantic and axiological belief systems'. See also Volosinov (1986: 109–59); Bakhtin (1968; 1984).

16 Goffman (1981: 144).

17 Barthes (1977).

18 The sentence used in this example is based on one in a Royal Society press release of 25 November 2003 which reads as follows: 'Lord May said: "If appropriately developed, GM crops could be used deliberately to improve the environment"', <http://www.royalsoc.ac.uk/templates/press/releasedetails.cfm?file=488.txt> (accessed 23 December 2003).

19 Tannen (1989: 98–133).

2 Scientists

1 Lord May of Oxford, Presidential Anniversary Address to the Royal Society 2002 'How to choose tomorrow, rather than just letting it happen, as scientific understanding advances', <http://www.royalsoc.ac.uk/royalsoc/AnniversaryAddress2002> (accessed 4 May 2003).

2 For more detailed analysis of the dangers of extraction, see O'Halloran (1997); Cook (1986).

3 The motto to which Lord May refers is *Nullius in verba*, words taken from Horace's lines:

> *nullius addictus iurare in verba magistri,*
> *quo me cumque rapit tempestas, deferor hospes.*
> [My words are not owned by any master,
> where the winds lead me, there I find home.]

(Horace, *Epistles*, I. i. 14–15)

They are taken to refer to the independence of science from any authority other than the truth.

4 Of the British National Corpus.

5 In this latter case, the initial coding must be done manually and will thus reflect to some degree the judgements and interpretations of the coders.

6 G. Cook, E. Pieri and P.T. Robbins, 'The presentation of GM crop research to non-specialists: a case study', funded by ESRC (R/000/22/3725), November 2001–November 2002. See Cook et al. (2003; 2004a); Robbins et al. (2004).

7 Cook et al. (2004a).

8 A claim contradicted by studies showing that people are, in certain contexts, generally ready to acknowledge and 'live with' uncertainty and the lack of control that it entails (Wynne 2002).

9 Gregory and Miller (1998); Hornig Priest (2001).

10 Later Chief Executive of the Medical Research Council. There was speculation in the press that he had been denied an honour at the intervention of Prince Charles. See *Observer*, 21 December 2003.

11 Quoted by George Monbiot in 'Beware the appliance of science', *Guardian*, 24 February 2000.

12 News release, Nobel House, London, 'Public to choose issues for GM debate – Beckett', 26 July 2002.

13 For example, in the case of GM, the EuroBarometer reports (BEPCAG 1997; INRA 2000).

14 Bucchi and Neresini (2002).

15 Grove-White et al. (1997), Marris et al. (2001).

16 'GM nation? The findings of the public debate', <http://www.aebc.gov.uk/aebc/reports/gm_nation_report_final.pdf> (accessed 20 November 2003).

17 Conducted to balance the possibility that those who turned up voluntarily to participate in the debate were partisan and unusually well informed.

18 For further comment on this view of NGO motives and its possible origin see Smith (2003: 227).

3 Journalists

1 G. Cook, E. Pieri and P.T. Robbins. 'The discourse of the GM food debate: how language choices affect public trust', funded by ESRC (RES/000/22/0132), January–December 2003. See Cook et al. (2004b).

2 Comprising 82 articles from the *Daily Mail*, 210 from the *Guardian*, 12 from the *Sun*, 142 from *The Times*.

3 For discussion of the relationship between linguistic features of newspapers and their readerships, see Jucker (1992).

4 Giddens (2002).

5 The broadsheet which became most anti-GM during this period, and which gave the issue most prominence, was probably, however, the *Independent*.

6 In the USA, a successful lawsuit was brought by three journalists against Fox International – also owned by Murdoch. They were dismissed from their jobs allegedly for refusing to make a news story about bovine growth hormone more favourable to Monsanto. See <http://www.poptel.org.uk/panap/latest/tv.htm> (accessed 2 January 2004); <http://www.btinternet.com/~clairejr/Articles/artic_12.html> (accessed 2 January 2004); Smith (2003: 183–98).

7 *Sun*, 20 May 2003.

8 *The Times*, 6 May 2003.

9 For further discussion of casual readings see O'Halloran (2003).

10 *Guardian*, 14 March 2003; see also Advisory Committee on Releases to the Environment, 'Advice on the implications of the farm-scale evaluations of genetically modified herbicide-tolerant crops', 13 January 2004, annex 2, pp. 15–17, <http://www.defra.gov.uk/environment/gm/fse/results/en-advice.pdf>.

11 The *Independent on Sunday*, 22 June 2003.

12 GM Science Review Panel, 'GM science review: first report', 2003, <http://www.gmsciencedebate.org.uk/report/default.htm#first> (accessed 2 February 2004).

13 Prime Minister's Strategy Unit, 'Field work: weighing up the costs and benefits of GM crops', 11 July 2003, <http://www.number-10.gov.uk/su/gm/downloads/gm_crop_report.pdf> (accessed 3 October 2003).

14 'GM crops: effects on farmland wildlife', 2003, <http://www.defra.gov.uk/environment/gm/fse/results/fse-summary.pdf> (accessed 10 December 2003); Firbank et al. (2003).

15 *The Times*, 8 July 2003, citing a 2002 article by Prince Charles in the *Evening Standard*.

16 *Guardian*, 17 February 2002.

17 The *Ecologist*, 17 February 2003. Significantly, two days after the Stop the War demonstration in London.

18 13 June 2003.

19 The *Independent on Sunday*, 22 June 2003.

20 *Guardian*, 6 September 2003.

21 The name Meacher is the 148th most frequent word in our newspaper corpus. It occurs 189 times, ahead of Bush (154 times), Blair (147 times), Monsanto (113 times) and Sainsbury (the man, not the shop, 123 times).

22 Unilever Chairman Niall FitzGerald, 'Facing the future – the UK food industry in a changing world', <http://www.fdf.org.uk/speeches/speech_150102.pdf> (accessed 5 January 2004).

4 Companies

1 <http://www.tesco.com/everyLittleHelps> (accessed 6 October 2003).

2 <http://www2.marksandspencer.com/thecompany/ourcommitmentto society/environment/info/food/gm/intro.shtml> (accessed 10 February 2004).

3 <http://www.sainsbury.co.uk/gm> (accessed 20 February 2004).

4 <http://www.co-op.co.uk/ext_1/Development.nsf/0/08cf9069352 cee5e0025683500432df0?OpenDocument> (accessed 20 February 2004).

5 ibid.

6 Fairclough (1992); Chouliaraki and Fairclough (1999).

7 For further analysis of biotech companies' self-presentation on environmental issues, see Robbins (2001).

8 <http://www.monsanto.com/monsanto/layout/default.asp> (accessed 14 September 2002).

9 Now shown on <http://www.monsanto.com/monsanto/layout/default.asp> (accessed 20 February 2004).

10 <http://www.monsanto.com/monsanto/layout/our_pledge/default.asp> (accessed 20 February 2004).

11 <http://www.monsanto.com/monsanto/layout/our_commitments/dialogue.asp> (accessed 14 September 2002).

12 Labov and Fanshel (1977: 100).

13 For further discussion, see Cameron (2000: 149–66).

14 'GM nation? The findings of the public debate', paragraph 131, <http://www.aebc.gov.uk/aebc/reports/gm-_nation_report_final.pdf>.

15 ibid, pp. 36–43; Corr Willbourn Research and Development, 'Qualitative research on a series of reconvened group discussions for the "narrow but deep" strand of the GM public debate', September 2003.

16 <http://www.monsanto.com/monsanto/layout/our_commitments/respect.asp> (accessed 14 September 2002).

17 <http://www.syngenta.com/en/social_responsibility/index.aspx> (accessed 20 February 2004).

5 Science and language

1 See Appendix 1.

2 There are many aspects of GM crops which could be judged aesthetically offensive. Genetically modified trees, for example, may have 'straighter trunks and less branches' (GeneWatch UK, 'Designer forests – the development of GM trees', briefing 16, September 2001).

3 See for example Widdowson (1979); Lemke (1990); Myers (1990); Halliday and Martin (1993); Kress et al. (1996); Graddol (1996).

4 See for example Dawkins (2003).

5 Dawkins (1976).

6 Although metaphor is used extensively in science (e.g. cosmic soup, charming particles) the use of this particular image is ironic in a book seeking explicitly to de-anthropomorphise evolution.

7 The description here is Popperian, on the assumption that this still constitutes the philosophy of science most widely accepted by practising scientists. See Popper (1959; 1972).

8 With some exceptions: see, for example, Wolpert (2004).

9 Rosch (1977); Lakoff (1987).

10 Guardian, 21 November 2002, <http://www.wholeagain.com/labeling. html> (accessed 20 December 2003).

11 Smith (2003: 244).

12 They are, respectively, a sexually potent adult male, a mature female, a castrated male, a male under the age of four, a female under the age of four, a juvenile of either sex.

13 i.e. members respectively of the Plant Kingdom (plantae) and the Animal Kingdom (animalia); see Wilson (1992: 157); Tudge (2000: 102–5).

14 Interview with Doug Parr, Chief Scientific Advisor, Greenpeace, 12 July 2002.

15 Asian Food Information Centre, <http://www.afic.org> (accessed 20 February 2004) and International Service for the Acquisition of Agri-biotech Application, 'Food biotechnology: a communication guide to improving understanding', <http://www.isaaa.org> (accessed 20 February 2004).

16 Washington Post, 1 January 2002, quoted in Smith (2003: 128).

17 A recombinant genetically engineered hormone which when injected into cows increases milk production by 10 to 15 per cent. For extensive discussion of the controversy around it see Smith (2003: Chapter 3).

18 ibid, p. 81.

19 ibid, p. 105; 'rbST' refers to artificial growth hormones given to cows.

20 In our machine-readable corpus of approximately one million words collected in 2002–3, 'genetic engineering' occurs only 133 times, 'genetic modification' 426 times, and 'GM' 4,174 times.

21 Orwell writes that in Newspeak 'It was perceived that in . . . abbreviating a name one narrowed and subtly altered its meaning, by cutting out the associations that would otherwise cling to it' (Orwell 1949: 263–4).

22 Whyte (2003: 61–3).

23 Smith (2003: 209).

24 ibid, p. 227. See also Appendix 1.
25 Smith (2003: 201).
26 ibid, p. 128.
27 Although there is substantial disagreement on the degree to which changes in communication technology (such as writing, print, computer-mediated communication) cause such effects. Compare, for example, the views of Ong (1982) with those of Olson and Torrance (1991).
28 See Macnaghten and Urry (1998: 202–9).

6 Key phrases

1 An increasingly preferred alternative in business discourse is 'enhanced'. Whereas 'improved' suggests that the product needed improving and therefore had faults, 'enhanced' suggests that it was good all along, but is now even better.
2 Monsanto, 'Fulfilling our pledge', 2000–1 report, p. 9, <http://www. monsanto.com/monsanto/content/media/pubs/2000/2000Pledge Report.pdf> (accessed 26 February 2004).
3 <http://www.monsanto.com/monsanto/content/media/press-kit/ presentations/6pledge.pdf> (accessed 26 February 2004).
4 <http://www.syngenta.com/en/about_syngenta/biotech.aspx> (accessed 26 February 2004).
5 Calculations of 'yield' will vary with definition of the term. Not surprisingly, a monoculture has a higher yield per hectare of that one crop than a mixed field, but that is not to say that the land is producing more food. Much traditional farming, especially in poorer countries, has mixed crops. See Five Year Freeze, 'Feeding or fooling the world: can GM really feed the hungry?', 2002, <http://www.fiveyearfreeze.org/Feed_ Fool_World.pdf> (accessed 26 February 2004).
6 The usual assumption that GM crop yields are higher than non-GM is contested in a number of studies: Soil Association Report, 'Seeds of doubt: North American farmers' experiences of GM crops', <http:// www.soilasociation.org/sa/saweb.nsf/getinvolved/geneng.html> (accessed 28 September 2002); Five Year Freeze, 'Feeding or fooling the world', p. 10, citing *inter alia* US Department of Agriculture, *Genetically Engineered Crops for Pest Management*, Washington DC: USDA Economic Research Service, 1999.
7 Five Year Freeze, 'Feeding or fooling the world'.
8 *Guardian*, 17 October 2002.
9 Top chefs are among those opposed to GM food. See 'Master chefs feed GM foods rebellion', *Guardian*, 13 October 2002, and 'The death of cooking', *Guardian Special Supplement*, 10 May 2003.
10 Cook et al. (2004b).
11 *Guardian*, 28 May 2003.
12 Ratified by 103 countries not including the USA.

13 *The Times*, 28 May 2003.
14 Juskevich and Guyer (1990).
15 Smith (2003: 93).
16 Advisory Committee on Releases to the Environment, 'Advice on the implications of the farm-scale evaluations of genetically modified herbicide-tolerant crops', 13 January 2004, p. 9, paragraph 32, <http://www.defra.gov.uk/environment/gm/fse/results/en_advice.pdf> (accessed 26 February 2004).
17 See Chapter 2, Note 3.
18 This is the case of research into genetics in general, not only GM agriculture. On the commercial interests of genetic scientists, see Lewontin (1993: 74) and Rifkin (1999: 55–6).
19 Carson [1962] (1999).
20 Revised for a second edition in 1831, the one still published today.
21 Shelley (1980: 112–15).
22 Richard Brinsley Peake's *Presumption; or the Fate of Frankenstein* (1823): see <http://meineseite.i-one.at/frankenstein/frankenstein-theatre_f.htm> (accessed 15 February 2004).
23 See 'GM nation?: the findings of the public debate', paragraph 56, <http://www.aebc.gov.uk.aebc/reports/gm_nation_report_final.pdf>: 'More frequently [than religious objections] people suggest that the human species has no right to use GM technology to alter the course of nature.'
24 See Williams (1983: 221). A notion echoed by the use of the name of the goddess Gaia to refer to the Earth (Lovelock 1979).
25 Nuffield Council on Bioethics, 'Genetically modified crops: the ethical and social issues', 1999, <http://www.nuffieldbioethics.org/publications/gmcrops/rep0000000179.asp> (accessed 26 February 2004).
26 Unless it was meant that they make no sense 'within scientific discourse', as opposed to for 'practising scientists'.
27 Nuffield Council on Bioethics, 'The use of genetically modified crops in developing countries', 2003, <http://www.nuffieldbioethics.org/file library/pdf/gm_crops_paper_final.pdf> (accessed 26 February 2004).
28 ibid, 3.7.
29 ibid, 3.8.
30 See Cook (2001: 149–65).
31 Williams (1983: 219).
32 For a much fuller discussion of the meanings of 'Nature' see Mcnaghten and Urry (1998).
33 See Chapter 2.
34 In the same month as the British Farm Scale Evaluation reported a negative impact on biodiversity of some GM crops, the pro-GM Food Standards Agency happened to report that a mycotoxin called fumonisin had been discovered in organic maize 'Toxin sparks organic scare', *Times Higher Educational Supplement* (31 October 2003).

35 Unilever Chairman Niall FitzGerald, 'Facing the future: the UK food industry in a changing world', <http://www.fdf.org.uk/speeches/speech_150102.pdf> (accessed 26 February 2004).
36 <http://www.connectotel.com/gmfood/cn100103.txt> (accessed 26 February 2004). See also *Guardian*, 10 January 2003.
37 'GM nation? The findings of the public debate', paragraph 63.
38 ibid, paragraph 102.
39 Quoted in Lambrecht (2001: 139).
40 Smith (2003: 252).
41 Thompson (1963); Sale (1995).
42 Sale (1995).
43 C.S. Prakesh of the Ag Bio Forum, quoted in Five Year Freeze, 'Feeding or fooling the world', p. 4.
44 See ibid.
45 Mcnaghten and Urry (1998: 147–62).

7 Metaphors and comparisons

1 See 'Afterword' by Linda Lear in the 1999 Penguin edition of *Silent Spring* (Carson [1962] 1999).
2 Nerlich (2003).
3 Sontag (1988).
4 Robert May, 'GM warriors have killed the debate', *Guardian*, 25 November 2003.
5 Report by the National Institute of Agricultural Botany, quoted in the *Guardian*, 3 January 2003.
6 'GM nation? The findings of the public debate', paragraph 72, <http://www.aebc.gov.uk.aebc/reports/gm_nation_report_final.pdf>.
7 Nuffield Council on Bioethics, 'Genetically modified crops: the ethical and social issues', 1999, 1.39, <http://www.nuffieldbioethics.org/publications/gmcrops/rep0000000179.asn>.
8 Five Year Freeze, 'Feeding or fooling the world: can GM really feed the hungry?', 2002, <http://www.fiveyearfreeze.org/Feed_Fool_World.pdf>.
9 Smith (2003).
10 Soil Association, 'Seeds of doubt: North American farmers' experience of GM crops', <http://www.grain.org/docs/seeds-of-doubt.pdf> (accessed 20 November 2003).
11 BBC Radio 4, 8 January 2003.
12 Hornig Priest (2001).
13 BBC2, 16 June 2002.
14 Interestingly, Bakhtin describes discourse with more than one voice using a plant metaphor, referring to it as 'hybrid'. See Chapter 1, Note 15.
15 Nuffield Council on Bioethics, 'Genetically modified crops: the ethical and social issues', 1.37–1.38.

16 *Catholic News*, August 2003, <http://www.cathnews.com/news/308/18. php> (accessed 20 January 2004).

17 'Genetically modified food: report of the Church of Scotland General Assembly', 11 May 1999, <http://www.srtp.org.uk/gmfood2.shtml> (accessed 18 May 2003).

18 Monsanto headquarters are in St Louis. According to the Pew Research Centre (<http://people-press.org/reports/display.php3?ReportID=167> (accessed 7 November 2003), 'Religion is much more important to Americans than to people living in other wealthy nations. Six-in-ten (59%) people in the U.S. say religion plays a very important role in their lives.' This contrasts with figures of 30 per cent or under in Canada, Europe and Japan.

19 <http://www.monsanto.com/monsanto/biotechnology/biobelt.html> (accessed 9 May 2001).

20 The term is applied both to Adam (Koran 2:30) and King David (Koran 38:26). For further commentary see Ruthven (1997: 49–59).

21 Esposito (2001).

22 <http://www.biotech-info.net/monsanto_on_btcorn.htm>l (accessed 4 February 2004); <http://www.syngenta.ca/en/bestpractices/index. asp>?nav=bp_ipm_basics> (accessed 4 February 2004).

23 Friends of the Earth, <http://www.foeeurope.org/press/2003/AB_14_ October_GMO.htm> (accessed 4 February 2004).

24 Rifkin (1999: 34–5).

25 Thomas Eisner, 'Chemical ecology and genetic engineering: the prospects for plant protection and the need for plant habitat conservation', paper given at Symposium on Tropical Biology and Agriculture, St Louis, Miss., organised by Monsanto, 1985, quoted in Rifkin (1999).

26 The comparison of genes to books permeates genetics, though it has many limitations. For a critique, see Cook (2000: 141–4).

27 Rifkin (1999: 34).

8 Public politics

1 Much work has been done on different national reactions to biotechnology. See for example Marris et al. (2001); papers in the journal *Public Understanding of Science* (2002, 11/2); Gaskell et al. (1999).

2 This section describing the 'GM nation?' debate was written in collaboration with Elisa Pieri.

3 Including citizens' juries organised by local councils.

4 An independent body providing strategic advice to government on the impact of biotechnology on agriculture and the environment: AEBC, 'Crops on trial', September 2001, <http://www.aebc.gov.uk/aebc/pdf/ crops.pdf> (accessed 20 February 2004); AEBC, 'Advice on the conduct of a public debate', April 2002, <http://www.aebc.gov.uk/aebc/reports/ public_debate_advice.shtml> (accessed 20 February 2004).

5 Corr Willbourn Research and Development, 'A report on the Foundation Discussion Workshops conducted to inform the GM public debate', 2003, <http://www.gmnation.org.uk/docs/corrwillbourn.pdf> (accessed 20 February 2004).

6 Secretary of State for the Environment, Food and Rural Affairs Margaret Beckett agreed in principle to a public debate in May 2002, and set a time-scale and a budget in July 2002. The debate was launched in June 2003.

7 GM Science Review Panel, 'GM science review: first report', 2003, pp. 129–31, <http://www.gmsciencedebate.org.uk/report/default.htm #first> (accessed 20 February 2004), Prime Minister's Strategy Unit, 'Weighing up the costs and benefits of GM crops', 2003, <http:// www.strategy. gov.uk/files/pdf/gm_crop_report.pdf> (accessed 20 February 2004).

8 'GM nation? The findings of the public debate', <http://www.aebc.gov. uk/reports/gm_nation_report_final.pdf>.

9 ibid, pp. 6–8.

10 ibid, key message 4.

11 Cook et al. (2004b).

12 Farmers are an ambiguous category. On the one hand they have a vested commercial interest in changes to agriculture, and for this reason were included in a list of 'major players' at the beginning of Chapter 4. Here they are included with 'members of the public'. This is justified by the view, which they expressed themselves, that they are powerless recipients of decisions made by others.

13 For a more detailed account of this focus group research, see Cook et al. (2004b).

14 Lakoff and Johnson (1980).

15 US Newswire, Washington DC, 26 March 2003, quoted in Smith (2003: 50).

Appendix 1 Disputed facts

1 For a popular account see Ridley (2000).

2 See especially Smith (2003).

3 See especially Smith (2003) and Humphrys (2001: 195–207).

4 *Guardian*, 22 June 2002.

5 The Royal Society Policy Document, 'Genetically modified plants for food use and human health – an update', 2002, <http://www.royalsoc. ac.uk/files/statfiles/document-165.pdf> (accessed 8 April 2003).

6 *Guardian*, 17 July 2002.

7 By examining stools and colostomy bags of people who had and had not eaten GM food.

8 Genes inserted into GM plants to allow the identification of the uptake of genetic material.

9 *Independent on Sunday*, 22 June 2003.

10 World Health Organisation (WHO), *Vaccines, Immunization and Biologicals. Vitamin A Deficiency*, quoted in Five Year Freeze, 'Feeding or fooling the world: can GM really freed the hungry?', 2002, <http://www.fiveyear-freeze.org/Feed_Fool_World.pdf>.

11 This paragraph is based on J.M. Dunwell, 'Future prospects for transgenic crops', *Phytochemistry Review* 1 (2002): 1–12. As the title indicates, these are, at the time of writing, prospects for future development. Such is the speed of GM development, however, that these innovations may already be in production by the time you read this book.

12 *Guardian*, 12 June 2003.

13 Gordon Conway, President of the Rockefeller Foundation, quoted in Five Year Freeze, 'Feeding or fooling the world: can GM really freed the hungry?', 2002, p. 21.

14 For further discussion see ibid, pp. 20–4.

15 UNISON, 'GM crops, food production and world hunger', June 2000, <http://www.unison.org.uk/resources/doc_view.asn?did=20&pid=25> (accessed 2 February 2004), S. Dibb and S. Mayer, 'Biotech – the next generation. Good for whose health?', report by the Food Commission (UK) Ltd and GeneWatch UK, April 2000, p. 44, <http://www.foodcomm.org.uk/biotech_summary.htm> (accessed 2 Feburary 2004).

16 Warwick et al. (2003).

17 Lord May of Oxford, Presidential Anniversary Address to the Royal Society 2002, 'How to choose tomorrow, rather than just letting it happen, as scientific understanding advances', <http://www.royalsoc.ac.uk/royalsoc/AnniversaryAddress2002> (accessed 4 May 2003). May points to the example of the 'escaped' Australian aquatic weed *Crassula helmsii* which infests garden ponds in the UK, or the floating pennywort *Hydrocotyle ranunculoides* causing problems in marshes and levels. Neither is genetically modified.

18 Quist and Chapela (2001). For discussion of the effect of the Quist and Chapela controversy on public perceptions of GM, see Mayer (2003).

19 *Seeds of Doubt*, BBC Radio 4, 19 January 2003.

20 ibid.

21 *Guardian*, 14 October 2003.

22 The original research conducted at Iowa and Cornell universities suggested that butterflies died after eating milkweed dusted with GM pollen growing among GM corn. Later research by the US National Academy of Sciences suggested that the risk was negligible. For discussion of this and other research on the monarch butterfly see GM Science Review Panel, 'GM science review: first report', 2003, <http://www.gmsciencedebate.org.uk/report/default.htm> first (accessed 20 February 2004).

23 'GM crops: effects on farmland wildlife', 2003, <http://www.defra.gov.uk/environment/gm/fse/results/fse-summary.pdf> (accessed 10 December 2003); Firbank et al. (2003).

24 Report for the Department for Environment Food and Rural Affairs by The National Institute of Agricultural Botany, 'Monitoring large scale releases of genetically modified crops (EPG 1/5/84) incorporating report on Project EPG 1/5/30: monitoring releases of genetically modified crops', <http://www.defra.gov.uk/environment/gm/research/epg-1-5-84.htm> (accessed 20 February 2004).

25 'GM crops: effects on farmland wildlife'.

26 Five Year Freeze, 'Feeding or fooling the world'.

27 Laurence Belsie, staff writer for the *Christian Science Monitor*, quoted in 'Feeding or fooling the world'.

28 For two reasons: first, because maize has no wild relatives in Britain, and second because it does not need to be sprayed with a broad-spectrum herbicide as early as other GM crops.

29 <http://www.syngenta.com/en/social_responsibility/index.aspx> (accessed 20 February 2004).

BIBLIOGRAPHY

Bains, W. (1993) *Biotechnology from A to Z*, New York: Oxford University Press.

Bakhtin, M.M. (1968) *Rabelais and His World*, Cambridge, Mass.: MIT Press.

—— (1981) *The Dialogic Imagination: Four Essays by M.M. Bakhtin*, Austin, Texas: University of Texas Press.

—— (1984) *Problems of Dostoevsky's Poetics*, Manchester: Manchester University Press.

Barthes, R. (1977) 'The death of the author', in R. Barthes, *Image, Music, Text*, ed. S. Heath, London: Fontana, 142–9.

Bauer, M. (2002) 'Controversial medical and agri-food biotechnology: a cultivation analysis', *Public Understanding of Science* 11: 93–131.

Bauer, M. and Gaskell, G. (eds) (2002) *Biotechnology: the Making of a Global Controversy*, Cambridge: Cambridge University Press.

BEPCAG (Biotechnology and the European Public Concerted Action Group) (1997) 'Europe ambivalent on biotechnology', *Nature* 387: 845–7.

Bucchi, M. and Neresini, F. (2002) 'Biotech remains unloved by more informed', *Nature* 416: 261.

Cameron, D. (2000) *Good to Talk? Living and Working in a Communication Culture*, London: Sage.

Carson, R. [1962] (1999) *Silent Spring*, Harmondsworth: Penguin.

Chouliaraki, L. and Fairclough, N. (1999) *Discourse in Late Modernity: Rethinking Critical Discourse Analysis*, Edinburgh: Edinburgh University Press.

Coates, J. (1986) *Women, Men and Language*, London: Longman.

Cook, G. (1986) 'Text, extract and stylistic texture', in C. Brumfit and R. Carter (eds) *Literature and Language Teaching*, Oxford: Oxford University Press.

—— (2000) *Language Play, Language Learning*, Oxford: Oxford University Press.

—— (2001) *The Discourse of Advertising*, second edition, London: Routledge.

155

Cook, G., Pieri, E. and Robbins, P.T. (2003) 'The presentation of GM crop research to non-specialists: a case study: final report', Swindon: ESRC.

—— (2004a) ' "The scientists think and the public feels": expert perceptions of the discourse of GM food', *Discourse and Society* 15: 433–51.

—— (2004b) 'The discourse of the GM food debate: final report', Swindon: ESRC.

Dawkins, R. (1976) *The Selfish Gene*, Oxford: Oxford University Press.

—— (2003) *A Devil's Chaplain*, London: Weidenfeld & Nicolson.

Esposito, J.L. (ed.) (2001) *The Oxford Encyclopedia of the Modern Islamic World*, 4 vols, New York and Oxford: Oxford University Press.

Fairclough, N. (1992) *Discourse and Social Change*, Cambridge: Polity.

—— (2000) *New Labour, New Language?*, London: Routledge.

Firbank, L.G. et al. (2003) 'The implications of spring-sown genetically modi-fied herbicide-tolerant crops for farmland biodiversity: a commentary on the Farm Scale Evaluations of Spring Grown Crops', *Philosophical Trans-actions of the Royal Society (Biological Sciences)* 358(149): 1773–913.

Fishman, P. (1980) 'Conversational insecurity', in H. Robinson, W.P. Giles and P.M. Smith (eds) *Language: Social Psychological Perspectives*, Oxford: Pergamon Press, 127–32.

Gaskell, G., Allum, N.C., Bauer, M.W. and Durant, J. (1999) 'Worlds apart? The reception of genetically modified foods in Europe and the US', *Science* 285: 384–7.

Giddens, A. (2002) *Where Now for New Labour?*, Cambridge: Polity.

Goffman, E. (1974) *Frame Analysis: an Essay on the Organization of Experience*, Boston, Mass.: Northeastern University Press.

—— (1981) *Forms of Talk*, Oxford: Basil Blackwell.

Graddol, D. (1996) 'The development of scientific English', in D. Graddol, D. Leith and J. Swann (eds) *English: History, Diversity and Change*, London: Routledge/Open University, 171–9.

Gregory, J. and Miller, S. (1998) *Science in Public*, Cambridge, Mass.: Perseus.

Grove-White, R., Macnaghten, P., Mayer S. and Wynne, B. (1997) *Uncertain World: GM Organisms, Food and Public Attitudes in Britain*, Lancaster Univer-sity: Centre for the Study of Environmental Change.

Halliday, M.A.K. and Martin, J.R. (1993) *Writing Science*, London: Falmer.

Hodson, A. (1992) *Essential Genetics*, London: Bloomsbury.

Hornig Priest, S. (2001) *A Grain of Truth: the Media, the Public and Biotech-nology*, Lanham, Md.: Rowman & Littlefield.

Humphrys, J. (2001) *The Great Food Gamble*, London: Hodder & Stoughton.

INRA (2000) 'The Europeans and biotechnology. EuroBarometer report', Brussels: DG Research, ECOSA for EU.

Jucker, A.H. (1992) *Social Stylistics. Syntactic Variation in British Newspapers*, Berlin and New York: Mouton de Gruyter.

Juskevich, J.C. and Guyer, C.G. (1990) 'Bovine growth hormone: human food safety evaluation', *Science* 249: 875–84.

Kress, G., Ogborn, J., Martins, I., McGillicuddy, K. (1996) *Explaining Science in the Classroom*, Buckingham: Open University Press.

Labov, W. and Fanshel, D. (1977) *Therapeutic Discourse: Psychotherapy as Conversation*, New York: Academic Press.

Lakoff, G. (1987) *Women, Fire and Dangerous Things: What Categories Reveal about the Mind*, Chicago, Ill.: Chicago University Press.

Lakoff, G. and Johnson, M. (1980) *Metaphors We Live By*, Chicago, Ill.: University of Chicago Press.

Lambrecht, B. (2001) *Dinner at the New Gene Cafe: How Genetic Engineering Is Changing What We Eat, How We Live, and the Global Politics of Food*, New York: St Martin's Press.

Lemke, J. (1990) *Talking Science: Language, Learning and Values*, Norwood, NJ: Ablex.

Lewontin, R.C. (1993) *The Doctrine of DNA: Biology as Ideology*, Harmondsworth: Penguin.

Louw, B. (1993) 'Irony in the text or insincerity in the writer? The diagnostic potential of semantic prosodies', in M. Baker, G. Francis and E. Tognini-Bonelli (eds) *Text and Technology: In Honour of John Sinclair*, Amsterdam and Philadelphia, Pa.: Benjamins, 157–76.

Lovelock, J. (1979) *Gaia: A New Look at Life on Earth*, Oxford: Oxford University Press.

Macnaghten, P. and Urry, J. (1998) *Contested Natures*, London: Sage.

Marris, C., Wynne, B., Simmons, P. and Weldon, S. (2001) *Public Perceptions of Biotechnologies in Europe. Final Report of the PABE Research Project*, Lancaster: University of Lancaster.

Myers, G. (1990) *Writing Biology. Texts in the Social Construction of Scientific Knowledge*, Madison, Wisc.: University of Wisconsin Press.

Nerlich, B. (2003) 'Tracking the fate of the metaphor silent spring in British environmental discourse: towards an evolutionary ecology of metaphor', *Metaphorik* <http://www.metaphorik.de/04/nerlich.pdf> (accessed 10 January 2004).

O'Halloran, K.A. (1997) 'Why Whorf has been misconstrued in stylistics and critical linguistics', *Language and Literature* 6: 163–80.

—— (2003) *Critical Discourse Analysis and Language Cognition*, Edinburgh: Edinburgh University Press.

Olson, D.R. and Torrance, N. (1991) *Literacy and Orality*, Cambridge: Cambridge University Press.

Ong, W.J. (1982) *Orality and Literacy*, London: Routledge.

Orwell, G. (1949) *Nineteen Eighty-Four*, Suffolk: Chaucer Press.

Popper, K. (1959) *The Logic of Scientific Discovery*, London: Hutchinson.

—— (1972) *Objective Knowledge*, Oxford: Oxford University Press.

Quist, D. and Chapela, I.H. (2001) 'Transgenic DNA introgressed into traditional landraces in Oxaca, Mexico', *Nature* 414: 541–2.

Ridley, M. (2000) *Genome: the Autobiography of a Species in 23 Chapters*, London: HarperCollins.

Rifkin, J. (1999) *The Biotech Century: How Genetic Commerce Will Change the World*, New York: Phoenix.

Robbins, P.T. (2001) *Greening the Corporation*, London: Earthscan.

Robbins, P.T., Pieri, E. and Cook, G. (2004) 'GM scientists and the politics of the risk society', in A.K. Haugestad and J.D. Wulfhorst (eds) *Future as Fairness: Ecological Justice and Global Citizenship*, Amsterdam and New York: Rodopi Press, 85–105.

Rosch, E. (1977) 'Human categorization', in N. Warren (ed.) *Advances in CrossCultural Psychology*, New York: Academic Press.

Rowell, A. (2003) *Don't Worry It's Safe to Eat: the True Story of GM Food BSE and Foot and Mouth*, London: Earthscan.

Ruthven, M. (1997) *Islam*, Oxford: Oxford University Press.

Sale, K. (1995) *Rebels Against the Future*, London: Addison Wesley.

Shelley, Mary [1918] (1980) *Frankenstein or the Modern Prometheus*, Oxford: Oxford University Press.

Sinclair, J.M. (1991) *Corpus, Concordance, Collocation*, Oxford: Oxford University Press.

Smith, J.M. (2003) *Seeds of Deception*, Fairfield, Ia.: Yes Books.

Sontag, S. (1988) *AIDS and Its Metaphors*, Harmondsworth: Penguin.

Tannen, D. (1989) *Talking Voices: Repetition, Dialogue, and Imagery in Conversational Discourse*, Cambridge: Cambridge University Press.

—— (1992) *You Just Don't Understand: Women and Men in Conversation*, London: Virago.

Thompson, E.P. (1963) *The Making of the English Working Class*, London: Vintage.

Tudge, C. (2000) *The Variety of Life*, Oxford: Oxford University Press.

Volosinov, V.N. (name used by M.M. Bakhtin) (1986) *Marxism and the Philosophy of Language*, Cambridge, Mass.: Harvard University Press.

Warwick, S.I. et al. (2003) 'Hybridisation between transgenic *Brassica napus L.* and its wild relatives: *Brassica rapa L.*, *Rahanus raphanistrum L.*, *Sinapsis arvensis L.*, and *Erucastrum gallicum (Willd.) O.E. Schulz*', *Theoretical and Applied Genetics* 107: 528–39.

Whyte, J. (2003) *Bad Thoughts: A Guide to Clear Thinking*, London: Corvo.

Widdowson, H.G. (1975) *Stylistics and the Teaching of Literature*, London: Longman.

—— (1979) 'The description of scientific language' in H.G. Widdowson, *Explorations in Applied Linguistics*, Oxford: Oxford University Press.

—— (2004) *Text, Context, Pretext: Critical Issues in Discourse Analysis*, Oxford: Blackwell.

Williams, R. (1983) *Keywords*, London: Collins Fontana.

Wilson, E.O. (1992) *The Diversity of Life*, London: Penguin.

Wolpert, L. (2004) 'Expertise required', *Times Higher Education Supplement*, 19 December.

Wynne, B. (2002) 'Risk and environment as legitimatory discourses of technology: reflexivity inside out', *Current Sociology* 50(3): 459–77.

INDEX

Bold indicates the most significant references to the entry.

Entries referring to a note are indicated by the page number followed by the letter 'N'.